BALI Unveiled

BALI Unveiled

The Secrets of Balinese Cuisine

Heinz von Holzen

mc Marshall Cavendish Cuisine

BALI Unveiled

The publisher wishes to thank **Mr. Fred B. Eisman** for writing the anecdotes included in this book, **P.T. Jenggala Keramik, Bali** for the loan and use of their tableware, and the staff at **Bumbu Bali, Balinese Restaurant & Cooking School** and **Rumah Bali, Balinese Village**, for their dedication and assistance throughout the length of the photography session.

Chef's Assistant	: I. Made Suriana
Editor	: Lydia Leong
Art Direction/Designer	: Lynn Chin Nyuk Ling
Photographer	: Heinz von Holzen

First published in 2004
Reprinted 2007, 2008

Copyright © 2004 Marshall Cavendish International (Asia) Private Limited
Published by Marshall Cavendish Cuisine
An imprint of Marshall Cavendish International
1 New Industrial Road, Singapore 536196

Other Marshall Cavendish Offices:

Marshall Cavendish Ltd. 5th Floor, 32-38 Saffron Hill, London EC1N 8FH, UK • Marshall Cavendish Corporation. 99 White Plains Road, Tarrytown NY 10591-9001, USA • Marshall Cavendish International (Thailand) Co Ltd. 253 Asoke, 12th Flr, Sukhumvit 21 Road, Klongtoey Nua, Wattana, Bangkok 10110, Thailand • Marshall Cavendish (Malaysia) Sdn Bhd, Times Subang, Lot 46, Subang Hi-Tech Industrial Park, Batu Tiga, 40000 Shah Alam, Selangor Darul Ehsan, Malaysia

Marshall Cavendish is a trademark of Times Publishing Limited

National Library Board Singapore Cataloguing in Publication Data

Holzen, Heinz von.
Bali unveiled :- the secrets of Balinese cuisine / Heinz von Holzen. – Singapore :- Marshall Cavendish Cuisine,- c2007.
p. cm.

ISBN-13 : 978-981-261-373-8
ISBN-10 : 981-261-373-0

1. Cookery, Balinese. 2. Cookery, Indonesian. I. Title. II. Title: Secrets of Balinese cuisine

TX724.5.I5
641.595986 — dc22   SLS2006039928

Printed in Singapore by KWF Printing Pte Ltd

Dedication

To Bali who has given me everything, making me a wiser and perhaps even a better person. With this book I would like to thank Bali and the world's kindest people for sharing their secrets with me and allowing me to share authentic Balinese cuisine with the world.

To my beautiful wife, Puji, who has bore us our beloved son, Fabian, and supported and encouraged me time after time through all the many seemingly impossible ideas which have laid the foundation for the culinary and cultural activities we undertake today.

Acknowledgements

I thank my mother-in-law, who is a terrific Balinese cook, for her patience in helping me prepare many dishes included in this book over and over again. As a foreigner to Bali, my Balinese family has not only accepted me wholeheartedly, but they have also given me the respect and support which contributed greatly to making our many ventures so successful.

To our great friend and partner, I. Nyoman Wijana, his family and the village of Sading, who ensured that the spiritual aspect of our lives remains in harmony with God and nature.

My deepest gratitude goes to Mr. Fred B. Eisman who shared with me his experience and research from over 40 years of being here in the southern part of Bali, contributing greatly to the colour of this book with his anecdotes and stories.

Finally, to the world's greatest team in Bumbu Bali, Balinese Restaurant and Rumah Bali, Balinese Village, which stood with me as only friends do. There is literally not a page in this book, which has not been influenced by their loyal, efficient and effortless assistance.

In sadness, I would like to remember Mr. Brent Hesselyn, the founder of Jenggala Keramik, whom we lost in a tragic dive accident. Without his guidance and support, our Balinese food venture would never have become a reality. All the dishes in this book are presented on Jenggala Keramik's fabulous table and chinaware.

Contents

72

Sates

82

Soups

92

Meats

150

Soy Beans & Eggs

156

Rice

170

Snacks

Introduction

Bali is a very small island, with an area of 5,700 sq km. Starting at any point in Bali, it is impossible to travel in a constant compass direction for more than 145 km before you reach the seashore. It is understandable therefore that visitors often make the assumption that the patterns of culture in Bali are uniform from place to place, since it is such a small island. Yet, nothing could be further from the truth—Bali's culture varies considerably from one place to the next.

Within the pages of this book, you will not find Balinese food commonly served at hotels and restaurants. The foods served in such establishments are usually prepared with the tastes and eating habits of foreign tourists in mind. As we shall see, such tastes and eating habits are quite different from those of the average Balinese person. We will take you on a journey into Balinese villages and homes and give you an insight into the ordinary everyday life of the Balinese people. The recipes featured here reflect true Balinese flavours and are not modified in any way to suit the palate of foreigners.

The Balinese people are mainly Hindu, with a small percentage being Muslim, Buddhist and Christians. Balinese life is thus almost inseparably linked with Hinduism, and the normal course of events inevitably includes the preparation of food in connection with Hindu religious beliefs.

Balinese Attitudes Toward Food

To the Balinese, food contains the mysterious power of sustaining life and death is inevitable without it. And since life comes from God, food must be part of the gift of life from God. Indeed, food is commonly referred to as *merta*, meaning "blessing from God", "livelihood" or "existence". As such, all aspects of food handling, from the sowing to the growing, the harvesting and transportation to the market, to the selling, buying, cooking, eating and use of the food in offerings, are actions that are related to God and the worship of God.

The offering of food to God is called *banten jotan*. Cooked food is offered before it is eaten. Even if away from home, a devout Balinese Hindu will place a little of the food on a banana leaf on the ground, say a short prayer and waft the prayer away from himself or herself toward God and the spirits. If the devotee has a drink, be it coffee, tea or even a soft drink, a little of it will also be poured on the ground as an offering.

While most Balinese understand the importance of eating a balanced diet, many are unable to afford one, since meat is expensive. Children are also encouraged to drink fresh milk, but milk is also largely unaffordable. Because of this financial limitation, food is chosen, cooked and eaten primarily based on affordability and taste.

Eating Habits

Eating is not a social activity in Bali. People eat simply to satisfy their hunger. Thus, eating is usually done alone, even when there are others nearby. Meals at home are usually the same from day to day and from meal to meal, changing only with the seasonal availability of the food items, their prices and perhaps the whim of the cook. A big bowl of rice remains the constant centrepiece.

After food is cooked, it may simply be left covered on a table or placed in a special basket called a *kerenjang gantung*, which is hung from the ceiling of the kitchen. Members of the household then help themselves to it whenever they are hungry. No effort is made to reheat or keep the food warm, although hot food is preferred, since the practice of eating separately, when the spirit moves, makes it impractical.

Invitation for Meals

The Balinese do not invite guests in advance to a meal at home in the way that Westerners might organise a dinner party. Should visitors drop in to discuss important matters or just to chat, they are served coffee or tea and a snack, but such business is never transacted over meals. If guests are present during meal times, however, the host will extend a polite invitation for them to eat together. Although this offer will always be routinely declined, it is always made.

Selamat Makan (Enjoy Your Meal)

When the Balinese are ready to eat, they put a heap of cooked rice on a plate and add a small quantity of each of the two or three side dishes provided to go with the rice. Side dishes may be fish, meat, vegetables or soy bean products such as *tempe* (fermented soy bean cakes) or bean curd. Having filled their plate, the Balinese then retreat to a favourite spot nearby on their own, and eat quickly, whether squatting, sitting or standing. The Balinese eat without cutlery, using only their right hand. The left hand is considered unclean because it is used for ablutions.

The exact way in which food is put into the mouth depends on whether the rice is steamed (*nasi kuskus*) or boiled (*nasi jakan*). Steamed rice is not sticky and can be easily moulded with the fingers into a convenient shape for pushing or throwing into the mouth. Boiled rice is usually quite sticky and cannot be as easily moulded. Instead, it is pushed with the tip of the fingers and thumb into a pyramid shape and then put into the mouth.

In those parts of Bali where rice is not readily available, other starchy foods are eaten, such as cassava or taro.

Nasi Campur (Mixed Rice)

In a sense, *nasi campur* refers to the rice and side dishes that the Balinese eat all the time. However, this term is usually used with reference to the dishes that one buys at a *warung* (stall). Most warungs that serve 'rice' (that is, a meal) have a glass display case in which servings of various pre-cooked dishes are placed. There is almost always fried chicken and usually some sort of meat, vegetables and sauces. Fried *tempe* (fermented soy bean cakes) and fried peanuts are standard fare. An order of *nasi* (rice) will include a scoop of rice from out of a big basket and small portions of each of the dishes on display plus a dollop of *sambal* (spicy chilli paste). Customers may request to omit certain ingredients or include an extra snack, although additions will cost extra. Some of the most well-known *warung nasi* (rice stalls) are crowded with people during midday.

Warung nasi do a thriving business in *nasi bungkus*, which just means *nasi campur* packed to be eaten elsewhere. The packaging is almost invariably a banana leaf or more commonly, two banana leaves layered and folded into a cone. The filled cone is then secured with a sliver of bamboo. Groups going on picnics or to some faraway temple for worship often take along huge baskets full of *nasi bungkus* for consumption after prayers.

Spice Pastes & Basic Recipes

Visitors to Bali seem to have the mindset that Balinese food is invariably hot. Guidebooks to Bali also contribute to this belief by employing the adjective "fiery" to describe the local dishes. In my opinion, there are only a few Balinese dishes within the entire cuisine that would probably be too spicy for the Western palate. There are plenty of spices in daily use and some of them have very strong effects, but these spices are not normally mixed in with the food while it is being cooked. Rather, a ground mixture or spicy chilli paste (*sambal*) is provided on the side so that the diner may choose to add as much or as little as he or she wishes. Balinese dishes are certainly not spicy, but spiced.

A visit to the local markets will help one become familiar with the great many varieties of roots, onions and garlic used in everyday cooking. The large multilevel market in Denpasar has most of its second floor devoted to selling spices. These spices are displayed in enormous baskets or piled high, and people come from all over south Bali to make their purchases because the prices are lower there. One important thing to keep in mind when choosing spices is that the appearance, aroma, flavour, texture and effectiveness of the spice are highly variable. Factors such as when it was harvested, the weather and the soil condition, among others will affect quality, so expect great variations and judge accordingly.

In Bali, every cooking process starts with the grinding of various spices. The resulting paste is known as *bumbu* or *base*. Most Balinese housewives don't buy spices individually. They purchase *base genep* (complete spice paste) by weight. *Base genep* consists of eight spices: shallots, galangal, lesser galangal, ginger, garlic, turmeric, chilli and candlenuts. In this book, we have streamlined the many spice mixtures prepared in Bali and have enclosed five basic recipes for vegetables, seafood, chicken, beef and meats with strong flavours such as pork, duck and lamb. You may prepare these spice pastes in large amounts and store them in the refrigerator for use as required.

Preparation for Social Events

Large scale ceremonies almost always translate into big feasts in Bali. In Jimbaran, in the southern part of Bali, preparation for such events begin with the helpers gathering in a central location, frequently the *bale banjar* (town meeting hall), the evening before, to chop up the spices. This process, known as *ngeracik basa*, meaning "mix", lasts about two hours, with a break for coffee and snacks in between.

If the ceremony is not a family affair, that is, if it takes place outside the home, it is strictly a male activity, although women are usually present to serve snacks and collect the chopped spices. The women have another duty. They cook the rice which must be ready by dawn the following day.

The men sit cross-legged on coconut leaf mats, either on the floor or on a raised table, in two long rows. They face each other with chopping boards, usually borrowed from the *banjar*, in between them. Each man brings his own knife, called a *berang*. It is usually large, almost like a cleaver, but with a very sharp point. The spices are delivered in woven coconut leaf baskets and are prepared as appropriate. Every helper knows exactly what to do because they have done it many times over.

Dressed in traditional formal Balinese costume consisting of a *sarung* with a sash tied around the waist, the men enjoy the opportunity for this social gathering. Often, a jug of *arak* (rice wine) is passed around to liven spirits. The tek-tek-tek sound of the knives on the cutting boards can be heard from a long distance away and it is an unforgettable part of Balinese village life.

The men return home when the preparation of the spices is complete. They get a few hours of sleep and then meet again shortly after midnight to cut up and prepare the meat for the feast. In the south of Bali, it is always turtle meat and in the other parts of Bali, it is always pork. Turtle meat does not keep long, so it must be consumed soon after it is cooked, around dawn. The spices are mixed by one or more of the men who are acknowledged to be so-skilled. Many Balinese dishes have subtle flavours, but there is nothing dainty about ceremonial cooking. During a typical village ceremony, food is prepared for approximately 700 people, including the helpers and their families. For this purpose, at least 55 kg of spices would be used.

Basic Spice Paste
Base Gede

Ingredients

Large red chillies	300 g, halved, seeded and sliced
Shallots	500 g, peeled and sliced
Garlic	100 g, peeled and sliced
Galangal	75 g, peeled and chopped
Ginger	75 g, peeled and sliced
Lesser galangal	100 g, peeled and sliced
Turmeric	175 g, peeled and sliced
Candlenuts	75 g
Dried prawn (shrimp) paste	2 Tbsp, roasted
Coriander seeds	2 Tbsp, crushed
Black peppercorns	1 Tbsp, crushed
Nutmeg	$1/4$ tsp, freshly grated
Cloves	8, crushed
Coconut oil	150 ml
Water	250 ml
Salt	$3/4$ tsp

Method

- Combine all ingredients except water and salt in a stone mortar or food processor and grind coarsely.

- Place ground ingredients in a heavy saucepan and simmer over medium heat for approximately 1 hour or until water is evaporated and paste takes on a golden colour. Cool before using or storing in the refrigerator.

Spice Paste for Vegetables
Base Jukut

Ingredients

Large red chillies	250 g, halved, seeded and sliced
Bird's eye chillies	25 g, sliced
Shallots	100 g, peeled and sliced
Garlic	100 g, peeled and sliced
Galangal	100 g, peeled and thinly sliced
Turmeric	100 g, peeled and sliced
Lesser galangal	100 g, peeled and sliced
Candlenuts	200 g
Coriander seeds	1 Tbsp, crushed
White peppercorns	$1/2$ Tbsp, crushed
Dried prawn (shrimp) paste	1 Tbsp, roasted and crumbled
Vegetable oil	150 ml
Salam leaves	2
Lemon grass	2 stalks, bruised
Salt	$3/4$ Tbsp
Water	250 ml

Method

- Combine all ingredients except *salam* leaves, lemon grass, salt and water in a stone mortar or food processor and grind coarsely.

- Place ground ingredients in a heavy saucepan, add remaining ingredients and simmer over medium heat for approximately 1 hour or until water is evaporated and paste takes on a golden colour. Cool before using or storing in the refrigerator.

Spice Paste for Beef
Base be Sampi

Ingredients

Large red chillies	250 g, halved, seeded and sliced
Bird's eye chillies	40 g, finely sliced
Garlic	50 g, peeled and sliced
Shallots	200 g, peeled and sliced
Ginger	50 g, peeled and sliced
Galangal	150 g, peeled and chopped
Candlenuts	100 g
Black peppercorns	2 Tbsp, crushed
Coriander seeds	2 Tbsp, crushed
Palm sugar	40 g, chopped
Coconut oil	150 ml
Salam leaves	3
Water	250 ml
Salt	³/₄ Tbsp

Method

- Combine all ingredients except *salam* leaves, water and salt, in a stone mortar or food processor and grind coarsely.

- Place ground ingredients in a heavy saucepan, add remaining ingredients and cook over medium heat for approximately 1 hour or until all water is evaporated and paste takes on a golden colour. Cool before using or storing in the refrigerator.

Spice Paste for Chicken
Base be Siap

Ingredients

Bird's eye chillies	50 g, finely sliced
Shallots	225 g, peeled and sliced
Garlic	125 g, peeled and sliced
Lesser galangal	50 g, peeled and sliced
Galangal	60 g, peeled and sliced
Turmeric	125 g, peeled and sliced
Candlenuts	100 g
Palm sugar	50 g, chopped
Coconut oil	150 ml
Lemon grass	2 stalks, bruised
Salam leaves	3
Water	250 ml
Salt	³/₄ Tbsp

Method

- Combine all ingredients except lemon grass, *salam* leaves, water and salt, in a stone mortar or food processor and grind coarsely.

- Place ground ingredients in a heavy saucepan, add remaining ingredients and cook over medium heat for approximately 1 hour or until all water is evaporated and paste takes on a golden colour. Cool before using or storing in the refrigerator.

Spice Paste for Seafood
Base be Pasih

Ingredients

Large red chillies	450 g, halved, seeded and sliced
Garlic	50 g, peeled and sliced
Shallots	225 g, peeled and sliced
Turmeric	175 g, peeled and sliced
Ginger	100 g, peeled and sliced
Candlenuts	125 g
Tomatoes	200 g, halved and seeded
Coriander seeds	2 Tbsp crushed
Dried prawn (shrimp) paste	2 Tbsp, roasted
Coconut oil	150 ml
Tamarind pulp	2¹/₂ Tbsp
Salam leaves	3
Lemon grass	2 stalks, bruised
Salt	³/₄ Tbsp
Water	250 ml

Method

- Combine all ingredients except tamarind pulp, *salam* leaves, lemon grass, salt and water in a stone mortar or food processor and grind coarsely.

- Place ground ingredients in a heavy saucepan, add remaining ingredients and simmer over medium heat for approximately 1 hour or until water is evaporated and paste takes on a golden colour. Cool before using or storing in the refrigerator.

Spiced Tomato Sauce
Sambel Tomat

This spicy sauce makes an ideal condiment for grilled fish.

Ingredients

Coconut oil	200 ml
Shallots	200 g, peeled and sliced
Garlic	100 g, peeled and sliced
Large red chillies	375 g, seeded and sliced
Bird's eye chillies	375 g, whole
Palm sugar	50 g, chopped
Dried prawn (shrimp) paste	1¹/₂ Tbsp, roasted
Tomatoes	750 g, peeled and seeded
Salt	to taste
Lime juice	1 Tbsp

Method

- Heat oil in a heavy saucepan, add shallots and garlic and sauté until golden.

- Add chillies and continue to sauté over high heat until chillies are soft. Add palm sugar and prawn paste and sauté until sugar caramelises. Finally add tomatoes and sauté until tomatoes are soft.

- Set aside to cool then grind in a stone mortar or purée coarsely in a food processor. Season to taste with salt and lime juice.

Note:
Cooking the ingredients over high heat while stirring continuously helps to preserve the red colour of the sauce.

These two sauces are delicious with meat sates and can also be used as a dressing for vegetable salads. One uses coconut milk, the other water. Always serve sate sauces warm.

Sate Sauce
Base Sate

Ingredients

Bird's eye chillies	6, sliced
Garlic	5 cloves, peeled and sliced
Lesser galangal	50 g, peeled and sliced
Peanuts (groundnuts) with skin	500 g, deep-fried or roasted golden brown
Palm sugar	50 g, chopped
Sweet soy sauce	4 Tbsp
Lime juice	1 Tbsp
Water	0.5 litre
Salt	a pinch

Method

- Put chillies in a stone mortar and grind into a very fine paste. Add garlic, lesser galangal and peanuts and grind again into a very fine paste.

- Add palm sugar, sweet soy sauce, lime juice and gradually add water. Slowly work this base into a creamy dressing by adjusting with water. Season to taste with salt.

Note:
This sauce can also be prepared using a food processor, but the real flavour will only be achieved by working a little harder with a stone mortar.

Sate Sauce with Coconut Milk
Base Sate

In most tourist-oriented hotels and restaurants, this sauce is served together with sate as a dipping sauce. Funny enough, the Balinese would never serve a dipping sauce with their sates, as sates are already marinated and do not require additional sauce. Instead, they dip their sates in a mixture of salt and chopped chillies.

Ingredients

Peanuts (groundnuts) with skin	500 g, deep-fried or roasted golden brown
Garlic	5 cloves, peeled and sliced
Bird's eye chillies	6–10, sliced
Lesser galangal	50 g, peeled and sliced
Coconut milk	1.5 litres
Sweet soy sauce	4 Tbsp
Palm sugar	50 g, chopped
Kaffir lime leaves	2, torn
Lime juice	1 Tbsp
Salt	a pinch
Fried shallots	1 Tbsp (see pg 37)

Method

- Combine peanuts, garlic, chillies and lesser galangal in a food processor and purée, or grind until very fine in a stone mortar.

- Place ground paste in a heavy saucepan together with coconut milk, sweet soy sauce, palm sugar and lime leaves. Bring to the boil, reduce heat and simmer uncovered, stirring frequently to prevent the sauce from sticking, for 10 minutes.

- Add lime juice and salt. Sprinkle with fried shallots just before serving.

Aubergine Salad
Sambel Terong

This salad has quite a kick and is delicious served with steamed rice and grilled fish and meats.

Ingredients

Coconut oil	2 Tbsp
Bird's eye chillies	1–3, finely sliced
Tomatoes	100 g, peeled, seeded and chopped
Lime juice	2 Tbsp
Salt	a pinch
Shallots	100 g, peeled and sliced
Aubergines (eggplants/brinjals)	150 g, sliced into fine strips

Method

- Combine coconut oil, chillies, tomatoes, lime juice and salt in a food processor or stone mortar and grind into a very fine paste.

- Add shallots and aubergines and mix well. Season to taste with salt.

Pickled Vegetables
Acar

This is another salad that goes well with grilled meats.

Ingredients

Water	250 ml
Sugar	250 ml
Rice or white vinegar	250 ml
Ginger	50 g, peeled and sliced
Lemon grass	1 stalk, bruised
Salt	a pinch
Cucumber	1, medium, peeled, seeded and cut into fine strips
Carrot	1, medium, peeled and cut into fine strips
Shallots	10, peeled and quartered
Bird's eye chillies	10

Method

- For the dressing, combine water, sugar, vinegar, ginger, lemon grass and salt in a saucepan and bring to the boil. Simmer for 1 minute and then allow to cool.

- Combine remaining ingredients and mix with dressing. Refrigerate for 24 hours before serving at room temperature.

Fried Garlic
Kesuna Goreng

Ingredients

Garlic	100 g, peeled and thinly sliced
Cooking oil	60 ml

Method

- Dry garlic on a paper towel.

- Heat oil until moderately hot, then add garlic and fry until lightly golden. Remove and drain then dry again on a paper towel before using or storing in an airtight container.

Fried Shallots
Bawang Goreng

Ingredients

Shallots	100 g, peeled and thinly sliced
Cooking oil	60 ml

Method

- Dry shallots on a paper towel.

- Heat oil until moderately hot, add shallots and fry until lightly golden. Remove and drain then dry again on a paper towel before using or storing in an airtight container.

Yellow Fried Shallots
Bawang Goreng Kuning

Ingredients

Shallots	100 g, peeled and thinly sliced
Turmeric	20 g, peeled and cut into fine strips
Cooking oil	60 ml

Method

- Dry shallots and turmeric on a paper towel.

- Heat oil until moderately hot, then fry shallots and turmeric until golden. Remove and drain then dry again on a paper towel before using or storing in an airtight container.

Yellow Fried Garlic
Kesuna Goreng Kuning

Ingredients

Garlic	100 g, peeled and thinly sliced
Turmeric	20 g, peeled and cut into fine strips
Cooking oil	60 ml

Method

- Dry garlic and turmeric on a paper towel.

- Heat oil until moderately hot then fry shallots and turmeric until lightly golden. Remove and drain then dry on paper towel before using or storing in an airtight container.

Fried Coconut with Turmeric
Saur

Ingredients

Coconut oil	**30 ml**
Spice paste for chicken	**30 g (see pg 31)**
Palm sugar	**1¹/₂ Tbsp**
Grated coconut	**120 g**
Salt	**a pinch**

Method

- Heat oil in a heavy saucepan. Add chicken spice paste and palm sugar and sauté until fragrant.

- Add grated coconut and sauté over low heat until coconut turns golden yellow. Allow to cool before adding salt.

Note:
This delicious fried coconut tastes best as a condiment when sprinkled on top of your rice or with vegetable dishes. Be careful not to add too much as the very strong coconut flavour can overpower the taste of the dish.

Turmeric Water

Ingredients

Turmeric	**150 g, peeled and finely chopped**
Water	**250 ml**

Method

- Combine turmeric with water in a food processor and grind until very fine. Allow it to rest for 5 minutes before straining it through a very fine sieve.

Sweet Tamarind Chilli Sauce
Base Rujak

Ingredients

Tamarind pulp	120 g
Warm water	125 ml
Palm sugar	250 g
Dried prawn (shrimp) paste	1 tsp, roasted and crumbed
Bird's eye chillies	6–8, finely sliced
Salt	$^1/_2$ tsp

Method

- Combine tamarind pulp and water and mix well. Allow tamarind to absorb all the liquid then strain it through a fine sieve to extract the juice. Discard the seeds.

- Combine remaining ingredients in a stone mortar or food processor and grind into a very fine paste. Slowly add tamarind juice and blend into a very smooth sauce. Season to taste with salt. Serve with cut unripe fruits (eg. mango or papaya) as a snack or as a starter to any meal.

Fried Chilli Dressing
Sambel Sere Tabia

Ingredients

Coconut oil	60 ml
Shallots	100 g, peeled and chopped
Garlic	75 g, peeled and chopped
Bird's eye chillies	25 g, finely sliced
Dried prawn (shrimp) paste	$^1/_2$ tsp, roasted and finely crumbled
Salt	a pinch

Method

- Heat oil in a frying pan (skillet), add shallots and garlic and sauté for 2 minutes.

- Add chillies and prawn paste and continue to sauté until golden. Season with salt.

Shallot and Lemon Grass Dressing

Sambel Matah

Ingredients

Shallots	40 g, peeled, each halved and finely sliced
Lemon grass	75 g, bruised, finely sliced and chopped
Garlic	20 g, peeled and finely chopped
Bird's eye chillies	30 g, finely sliced
Kaffir lime leaves	2, finely chopped
Dried prawn (shrimp) paste	$^1/_2$ tsp, roasted and finely crumbled
Lime juice	30 ml
Coconut oil	60 ml
Salt	a pinch or to taste
Ground black pepper	a pinch or to taste

Method

- Combine all ingredients except salt and pepper in a deep bowl and mix thoroughly for 5 minutes. Season to taste with salt and pepper.

Tip: Another way to make this dressing is by heating the oil in a saucepan, then cooking all the ingredients for 5 minutes over medium heat or until sauce is fragrant. Cool to room temperature before using.

Stock
Kuah

Ingredients

Chicken, beef, duck or pork bones	5 kg, chopped into 2.5-cm pieces
Spice paste	375 g (use according to type of stock. see pg 30–32)
Lemon grass	1 stalk, bruised
Lime leaves	3, torn
Large red chillies	2, bruised
Bird's eye chillies	3
Salam leaves	2
White peppercorns	1 Tbsp, coarsely crushed
Coriander seeds	1 Tbsp, crushed

Method

- Rinse bones until water is clear. Place in a stockpot and fill with water until bones are submerged. Bring to the boil over high heat, then drain and discard water.

- Wash bones again under running water and return bones to stockpot. Add 3 times as much water as bones and return to the boil. Reduce heat and skim off scum with a ladle as it accumulates at the surface.

- Add remaining ingredients and simmer stock over very low heat for 5–6 hours. If making pork stock, simmer only for 2 hours. It is important not to cover the stockpot during cooking, as it will make the stock cloudy. Strain stock. This recipe makes about 3 litres.

> Tip: Freeze the stock in small containers in the freezer, then thaw the required amount when needed.

Chilli Soy Sauce
Tabia Lalah Manis

Ingredients

Bird's eye chillies	15, finely chopped
Sweet soy sauce	125 ml
Light soy sauce	125 ml

Method

- Combine all ingredients and mix well just before it is required.

Palm Sugar Syrup

Ingredients

Palm sugar	375 g, chopped
Water	250 ml
Screwpine (*pandan*) leaf	1

Method

- Combine all ingredients in a saucepan. Bring to the boil and simmer for 10 minutes. Cool before using.

Vegetables & Salads

Plants and vegetables are likely to differ in taste and texture, and even appearance, depending upon how long ago they where harvested, the season, weather, soil and many other factors. As such, vegetables of a single species from various sellers might show considerable variation.

In Bali, every square metre of arable land is farmed. Green vegetables are often cultivated close to fruit trees and banana and coconut trees are almost everywhere. (As a result, banana and coconut have become important ingredients in many Balinese dishes.) Prior to the implementation of new rice (Balinese dwarf strains with high yield and short growing seasons), the Balinese cultivated a large variety of vegetables and leaves from edible plants right in their backyard, including starfruit, papaya, jackfruit, banana, cassava, yam, sweet potato, long beans, mung beans, bean sprouts, spinach, cabbage and peanuts (groundnuts).

Most of these fruit, vegetables, leaves or beans are simply steamed, cooled to room temperature, then mixed with coconut and spiced before serving with rice and other dishes. To the Balinese, these are salads. Salads, as known to Westerners, do not exist in Bali as the Balinese never eat raw vegetables with the exception of the occasional cucumber. The Asian concept of quickly stir-frying vegetables so as to heat them but maintain crispness also does not exist in Bali. Vegetables are always eaten well-cooked and limp or soft.

To make vegetable dishes more interesting, the Balinese mix the cooked vegetables with grated coconut. Such a mixture is called an *urab* and the vegetables are said to be *maurab* or *murab*. For example, *bayem murab* would refer to the vegetable, *bayem* (similar to spinach), mixed with grated coconut. If several vegetables are in the *urab*, then the name of the main vegetable would be used when referring to the dish.

The vegetable dish that is likely to be most familiar to foreigners is similar to the popular Indonesian dish known as *gado-gado*. The Balinese version is called *jukut pecel* or *jukut plecing*. The word *pecel* has two meanings. It either refers to squeezing something or to the vegetable mixture. The two meanings do not appear to be related, however, as making *jukut pecel* does not involve squeezing anything. The dish is simply a mixture of spices and one or more boiled vegetables such as water spinach, cabbage, long beans and bean sprouts.

Sellers of vegetable dishes are a common sight outside the larger markets in Denpasar. They often set up temporary stalls in the parking lots next to the markets, or spread their wares out on the pavement. They always attract a large crowd. Besides the standard dishes, some of these stalls also sell a dish called *cap cay*, an Indonesian dish that consists of Chinese-style, stir-fried vegetables, usually with some sort of meat or prawns (shrimp). I have been told that the word *cap* means "ten" and that *cay* means "vegetables", but I cannot confirm if this is true.

Another method of cooking vegetables is adding them to rice either while the rice is cooking or after it has been cooked. The former method is called *moran*, the latter *moreng*. To prepare *jukut moran*, cook the rice until the remaining time for cooking is approximately the time it takes the vegetables to cook. Put the vegetables in. To make *jukut moreng*, cook the rice and add a little water. Mix in whatever cooked vegetables are desired then add some grated coconut, coconut cream and a spice paste.

Some of the vegetables in the markets are recent introductions grown in response to the influx of tourists in Bali. These include beets, radishes, parsley, large white onions, celery and a kind of lettuce.

Cucumbers in Coconut Sauce

Timun Mesanten Serves 4

Ingredients

Coconut oil	30 ml
Shallots	30 g, peeled and sliced
Garlic	20 g, peeled and sliced
Large red chillies	2, seeded and sliced
Dried prawn (shrimp) paste	1/2 tsp, roasted and crumbled
Spice paste for vegetables	30 g (see pg 30)
Chicken or vegetable stock	250 ml (see pg 41)
Coconut cream	250 ml
Salam leaves	2
Bird's eye chillies	2, crushed (optional)
Cucumbers	2, peeled, seeded and sliced
Salt	a pinch
White peppercorns	1/4 tsp, crushed
Fried shallots	2 Tbsp (see pg 37)

Method

- Heat oil in heavy saucepan and sauté shallots, garlic and chillies for 2 minutes over low heat.

- Add dried prawn paste and spice paste and sauté for another minute or until fragrant. Pour in stock and coconut cream, add *salam* leaves and chillies and bring to the boil.

- Add cucumbers and bring sauce back to the boil. Reduce heat and simmer for 5 minutes or until cucumbers are done. Cucumbers should still be crunchy. Season to taste with salt and pepper and garnish with fried shallots.

Long Beans in Soy Dressing

Buah Kacang Mekuah Serves 4

Ingredients

Cooking oil	2 Tbsp
Garlic	20 g, peeled and sliced
Shallots	30 g, peeled and sliced
Large red chillies	2, seeded and sliced
Dried prawn (shrimp) paste	1/2 tsp, roasted and crumbled
Spice paste for vegetables	45 g (see pg 30)
Sweet soy sauce	45 ml
Light soy sauce	45 ml
Long beans	600 g, cleaned and blanched
Chicken or vegetable stock	250 ml (see pg 41)
Salt	to taste
Fried shallots	2 Tbsp (see pg 37)

Method

- Heat oil in heavy saucepan and sauté garlic, shallots and chillies for 2 minutes. Add dried prawn paste and spice paste and continue to sauté until fragrant.

- Add sweet and light soy sauces and long beans and sauté for another 1 minute.

- Add stock and bring to the boil. Braise long beans until tender. Season to taste with salt and garnish with fried shallots.

From top: Cucumbers in Coconut Sauce; Long Beans in Soy Dressing

Young Jackfruit Braised in Coconut Dressing

Jukut Nangka Mekuah Serves 4

Ingredients

Cooking oil	30 ml
Spice paste for vegetables	125 g (see pg 30)
Young green jackfruit	600 g, peeled, cleaned and cut into 2.5 x 1-cm pieces
Chicken or vegetable stock	1 litre (see pg 41)
Lemon grass	2 stalks, bruised
Salam leaves	2
Bird's eye chillies	3, bruised (optional)
Coconut cream	250 ml
Salt	a pinch
White peppercorns	2–3, crushed
Fried shallots	2 Tbsp (see pg 37)

Method

- Heat oil in a heavy saucepan and sauté spice paste until fragrant. Add jackfruit and continue to sauté for 2 more minutes. Pour in stock, add lemon grass, *salam* leaves and chillies and bring to the boil. Lower heat and simmer for 10 minutes or until jackfruit is 90 per cent soft.

- Add coconut cream and continue to simmer over very low heat until jackfruit is tender. Season to taste with salt and pepper. Garnish with fried shallots.

Vegetable Salad in Peanut Chilli Dressing

Serombotan Serves 4

Ingredients

Bean sprouts	100 g, blanched
Water convolvulus	100 g, cut into 2.5-cm lengths and blanched
Baby aubergines (eggplants/brinjals)	100 g, finely sliced
Soy beans	50 g, deep-fried
Black beans	100 g, blanched
Grated coconut	100 g

Dressing

Coconut oil	30 ml
Garlic	5 cloves, peeled and sliced
Large red chillies	4, seeded and sliced
Bird's eye chillies	10
Dried prawn (shrimp) paste	1 tsp, roasted
Peanuts (groundnuts) with skin	80 g, deep-fried until golden brown
Salt	to taste
Water	80 ml
Lime juice	extracted from 1 lime
Ground black pepper	to taste

Method

- Toss bean sprouts, water convolvulus, aubergines, soy beans, black beans and grated coconut together.

- For the dressing, heat oil in heavy saucepan, add garlic and chillies and sauté until chillies are soft. Add dried prawn paste and continue to sauté for 1 more minute. Leave to cool before placing in a food processor or stone mortar. Add half the peanuts and salt and grind mixture into a fine paste.

- Add water and lime juice then season to taste with more salt and pepper. Toss vegetable mixture and dressing well. Garnish with remaining peanuts.

Fern Tips in Garlic Dressing
Sayur Pakis Serves 4

Ingredients

Young fern tips	**400 g**
Garlic	**3 cloves, peeled and finely chopped**
Lesser galangal	**50 g, peeled and chopped**
Bird's eye chillies	**4–7**
Dried prawn (shrimp) paste	**1 tsp, roasted and finely crumbed**
Coconut oil	**30 ml**
Salt	**a pinch**
Black peppercorns	**2–3, crushed**

Method

- Blanch fern tips in boiling water for 1 minute then drain and cool under running water. Drain and dry thoroughly. Set aside.

- Place all remaining ingredients in a food processor or stone mortar and grind into a fine paste.

- Combine this mixture with the fern tips and mix well. Season to taste with salt and pepper. Serve at room temperature.

Water Spinach in Tomato Chilli Dressing
Pelecing Kangkung Serves 4

This delicious dish is often served with grilled seafood.

Ingredients

Water spinach or spinach	**500 g, cleaned and trimmed**

Dressing

Coconut oil	**30 ml**
Large red chillies	**100g, seeded and sliced**
Garlic	**20 g, peeled and sliced**
Dried prawn (shrimp) paste	**1/2 tsp**
Tomatoes	**175 g, peeled, seeded and sliced**
Salt	**a pinch**
Lime juice	**2 Tbsp**
Peanuts (groundnuts)	**2 Tbsp, roasted and chopped**

Method

- In a stockpot, bring 3 litres of water to the boil and stir in 2 Tbsp salt. Add spinach, stir well and bring water back to the boil then simmer for 2 minutes. Drain water and cool spinach in ice water. Drain and dry spinach well.

- For the dressing, heat oil in a frying pan (skillet). Add chillies, garlic and dried prawn paste and sauté over medium heat until chillies are soft. Set aside to cool then transfer ingredients into a food processor or stone mortar and grind into a very fine paste. Add tomatoes, salt and lime juice and continue grinding to make a very fine dressing.

- Just before serving, toss spinach and dressing and mix well. Season to taste with salt and sprinkle with chopped peanuts.

Note:
If you wish to increase the spiciness of this dish, simply add several sliced bird's eye chillies together with the large red ones.

Mixed Vegetables with Grated Coconut

Jukut Urab Serves 4

Ingredients

Cabbage	150 g, cut into 1.5-cm squares and blanched
Spinach	150 g, cut into 2.5-cm lengths and blanched
Long beans	150 g, cut into 2.5-cm lengths and blanched
Bean sprouts	150 g, blanched
Large red chillies	2, seeded and sliced
Grated coconut	300 g, lightly roasted
Fried shallots	3 Tbsp (see pg 37)

Dressing

Cooking oil	30 ml
Fried chilli dressing	4 Tbsp (see pg 39)
Kaffir lime leaves	3, finely chopped
Palm sugar	1 Tbsp, chopped
Lesser galangal	40 g, peeled and finely ground
Salt	a pinch
Black peppercorns	2–3, crushed

Method

- Mix dressing ingredients well.

- Combine vegetables, chillies and grated coconut and toss with dressing. Garnish with fried shallots.

Note:

This popular vegetable dish can also be prepared with a mixture of seaweed, spinach, beans and corn kernels. It makes a great accompaniment to stewed or grilled meats.

Vegetable Salad in Peanut Dressing

Pecelan Serves 4

Ingredients

Salt	a pinch
Ground black pepper	a pinch

Peanut Sauce

Peanuts (groundnuts) with skin	250 g, deep-fried until golden brown
Garlic	3 cloves, peeled and sliced
Bird's eye chillies	1–3, finely sliced
Lesser galangal	25 g, peeled and finely sliced
Sweet soy sauce	30 ml
Palm sugar	20 g, chopped
Salt	a pinch
Water	250 ml

Salad

Long beans	100 g, cut into 2.5-cm lengths and blanched
Bean sprouts	100 g, blanched
Spinach	100 g, cut into 2.5-cm lengths and blanched
Cabbage	100 g, thinly sliced and blanched

Garnish

Fried shallots	2 Tbsp (see pg 37)
Peanuts (groundnuts) with skin	2 Tbsp, deep-fried until golden brown and crushed

Method

- For the peanut sauce, combine all ingredients, except water in a food processor or stone mortar and grind until fine. Gradually add water until desired consistency is reached.

- Combine salad ingredients and mix well with peanut sauce. Season to taste with salt and pepper. Garnish with fried shallots and crushed peanuts.

Creamy Vegetable Salad

Jukut Antungan Serves 4

Ingredients

Spice paste for vegetables	125 g (see pg 30)
Coconut cream	125 ml
Chicken or vegetable stock	125 ml (see pg 41)
Green leafy vegetables	600 g, blanched
Yellow fried shallots	2 Tbsp (see pg 37)
Yellow fried garlic	2 Tbsp (see pg 37)
Bird's eye chillies	3, sliced and fried until golden brown
Lime juice	2 Tbsp
Salt	a pinch
Ground white pepper	a pinch
Fried shallots	2 Tbsp (see pg 37)

Method

- Combine spice paste and coconut cream in a food processor or stone mortar and grind until very fine. Place into a saucepan, add stock and ground paste and bring quickly to the boil, then set aside to cool.

- In a deep bowl, combine all ingredients, mix well and season to taste with more salt and pepper if necessary. Garnish with fried shallots.

Honeycomb Salad with Green Papaya

Lawar Nyawan Serves 4

Ingredients

Honeycomb	600 g, cleaned and cut into 5 x 5-cm squares
Green papaya	400 g, peeled, seeded and cut into matchstick-sized strips

Sauce

Cooking oil	30 ml
Spice paste for chicken	125 g (see pg 31)
Chicken stock	125 ml (see pg 41)
Coconut cream	125 ml
Fried garlic	2 Tbsp (see pg 37)
Palm sugar	1 Tbsp, finely chopped
Bird's eye chillies	2, sliced and fried until golden
Lime juice	2 Tbsp
Ground white pepper	a pinch
Salt	a pinch
Fried shallots	2 Tbsp (see pg 37)

Method

- In a heavy stockpot, bring 3 litres of lightly salted water to the boil, add honeycomb, bring back to the boil and simmer for 10 minutes. Drain and cool honeycomb in ice water. Drain again and dry honeycomb well. Chop evenly but not too fine. Set aside.

- Blanch papaya strips for 1 minute, then drain and cool in ice water. Drain and dry.

- For the sauce, heat oil in a frying pan (skillet), add spice paste and sauté until fragrant. Add stock and coconut cream and bring back to the boil. Simmer for 1 minute before cooling to room temperature.

- Combine honeycomb, papaya strips, sauce and remaining ingredients except fried shallots. Blend well and season to taste with more pepper and salt if necessary. Garnish with fried shallots.

From top: Creamy Vegetable Salad; Honeycomb Salad with Green Papaya

Green Vegetables with Corn
Don Kelor dan Jagung Serves 4

Ingredients

Shallots	50 g, peeled and sliced
Garlic	40 g, peeled and sliced
Bird's eye chillies	2–4, finely sliced
Turmeric	20 g, peeled and sliced
Ginger	20 g, peeled and sliced
Lesser galangal	10 g, peeled and sliced
Dried prawn (shrimp) paste	¹/₂ tsp, roasted
Coconut oil	1 Tbsp
Coconut cream	125 ml
Galangal	20 g, peeled sliced and bruised
Lemon grass	1 stalk, bruised
Salam leaf	1
Salt	a pinch
White peppercorns	2–3, crushed
Kelor or spinach leaves	400 g, blanched and drained
Canned corn kernels	200 g

Method

- Combine shallots, garlic, chillies, turmeric, ginger, lesser galangal and dried prawn paste in a food processor or stone mortar and grind coarsely.

- Heat oil in saucepan, add ground paste and fry until fragrant and golden brown. Pour in coconut cream, add galangal, lemon grass, *salam* leaf, salt and pepper. Bring to the boil and simmer for 5 minutes.

- Add vegetables and corn. Bring back to the boil and simmer again for 2 minutes. Season to taste with salt and pepper.

Note:
You may also use fresh corn kernels instead of canned corn kernels, but blanch them before use.

Tuna Salad with Shallots and Lemon Grass

Sambel be Tongkol *Serves 4*

Ingredients

Tuna steaks	4, each about 150 g
Spice paste for seafood	60 g (see pg 32)
Salt	a pinch
White peppercorns	2–3, finely crushed
Lime juice	1 Tbsp
Coconut oil	2 Tbsp
Shallot and lemon grass dressing	250 ml (see pg 40)

Method

- Season tuna steaks with spice paste, salt, pepper and lime juice.

- Heat oil in frying pan (skillet) and cook tuna steaks over medium heat, turning frequently until desired doneness. Set aside and allow to cool down before breaking tuna into small chunks.

- Place tuna into a mixing bowl, add shallot and lemon grass dressing and mix well. Season to taste with salt and pepper.

- Serve at room temperature with steamed rice or as a cocktail snack on top of deep-fried crackers (*krupuk*).

Beef Salad with Coconut
Serapa Sampi Serves 4

Ingredients

Beef topside	800 g, cut into 4 thick steaks
Beef liver	400 g, cut into 4 thick chunks
Spice paste for beef	125 g (see pg 31)
Beef or chicken stock	2 litres (see pg 41)
Coconut cream	250 ml
Fried garlic	2 Tbsp (see pg 37)
Bird's eye chillies	2, finely chopped
Palm sugar	1 Tbsp, finely chopped
Lime juice	1 Tbsp
Salt	to taste
Ground white pepper	to taste
Fried shallots	2 Tbsp (see pg 37)

Method

- Rub topside and liver evenly with half the spice paste and leave to marinate for 2 hours in the refrigerator.

- Bring stock to the boil then add marinated topside. Simmer until almost soft, then add liver and continue to simmer until both meats are tender. Allow to cool to room temperature in stock. When cooled, remove topside and liver and drain well. Cut into cubes of even sizes. Set aside. Reserve stock.

- For the dressing, sauté remaining spice paste in a saucepan until fragrant. Add 125 ml of reserved stock, bring to a simmer and add coconut cream. Bring back to the boil and simmer until sauce thickens slightly. Cool to room temperature and add all remaining ingredients except salt, pepper and fried sahllots.

- Combine meat and dressing and season to taste with salt and pepper. Garnish with fried shallots.

Green Papaya Salad with Prawns
Lawar Gedang Udang Serves 4

Ingredients

Green papaya	400 g, peeled, halved, seeded and cut into fine strips, then blanched
Grated coconut	120 g, roasted
Yellow fried shallots	2 Tbsp (see pg 37)
Yellow fried garlic	2 Tbsp (see pg 37)
Large red chillies	2, seeded and sliced
Bird's eye chillies	2 Tbsp, sliced and fried until golden brown
Kaffir lime leaves	2–3, finely chopped
Fried shallots	2 Tbsp (see pg 37)

Dressing

Cooking oil	30 ml
Spice paste for seafood	125 g (see pg 32)
Prawns (shrimps)	250 g, peeled and minced
Chicken or fish stock	125 ml (see pg 41)
Coconut cream	125 ml
Salt	a pinch
White peppercorns	2–3, crushed
Lime juice	2 Tbsp

Method

- Prepare dressing. Heat oil in heavy saucepan, add spice paste and sauté until fragrant. Add minced prawns and continue to sauté until meat changes colour.

- Stir in stock and coconut cream. Bring to the boil and simmer for 1 minute. Season to taste with salt, pepper and lime juice. Allow to cool to room temperature.

- In a deep bowl, combine all other ingredients except fried shallots and mix well with dressing. Garnish with fried shallots.

Shredded Chicken with Chillies and Lime

Ayam Pelalah Serves 4

This recipe offers a delicious way to use up any chicken left over from the previous meal. If using cooked chicken, omit roasting it as mentioned in this recipe.

Ingredients

Chicken	1, about 1.5 kg
Salt	1 Tbsp
Black peppercorns	2–3, finely crushed
Spice paste for chicken	200 g (see pg 31)
Salam leaves	2
Lemon grass	2 stalks, bruised
Kaffir lime leaves	2
Spiced tomato sauce	1 Tbsp (see pg 32)
Lime juice	3 Tbsp
Fried shallots	2 Tbsp (see pg 37)

Basting Mix

Spice paste for chicken	125 g (see pg 31)
Coconut oil	125 ml

Method

- Rub inside and outside of chicken with salt and pepper. Stuff 3 Tbsp spice paste, *salam* leaves, lemon grass and lime leaves inside chicken, then close opening with a *sate* skewer. Rub outside of chicken evenly with remaining spice paste.

- Combine ingredients for basting mix and have it ready to baste chicken frequently as it roasts.

- Place chicken on a wire rack in a preheated oven and roast at 220°C for 10 minutes, then turn heat down to 160°C and roast chicken until done and the juices run clear. Remove from oven and cool to room temperature.

- When cooled, peel and discard chicken skin. Debone chicken and shred meat by hand into fine strips. Reserve stuffing.

- Combine chicken strips with spiced tomato sauce, lime juice, fried shallots and chicken stuffing. Mix well and season to taste. Serve at room temperature with steamed rice.

Tip: As an alternative to this recipe, you can make Shredded Chicken with Shallot and Lemon Grass Dressing (*Ayam Sambel Matah*). Simply replace spiced tomato sauce with shallot and lemon grass dressing (see pg 40).

Shredded Chicken with Jackfruit
Jejeruk Ayam Serves 4

Ingredients

Chicken	1, about 1.5 kg
Salt	1 Tbsp
Black peppercorns	2–3, finely crushed
Spice paste for chicken	200 g (see pg 31)
Salam leaves	2
Kaffir lime leaves	2
Lemon grass	2 stalks, bruised
Young jackfruit	400 g, peeled, sliced in wedges and steamed
Coconut cream	125 ml
Grated coconut	60 g
Fried chilli dressing	2 Tbsp (see pg 39)
Lime juice	1 Tbsp
Fried shallots	2 Tbsp (see pg 37)

Basting Mix

Spice paste for chicken	125 g (see pg 31)
Coconut oil	125 ml

Method

- Season inside and outside of chicken with salt and pepper then fill chicken with 3 Tbsp spice paste, *salam* leaves, kaffir lime leaves and lemon grass. Close opening with a *sate* skewer. Rub outside of chicken evenly with remaining spice paste.

- Combine ingredients for basting mix and have it ready to baste chicken frequently as it roasts.

- Place chicken on a wire rack in a preheated oven and roast at 220°C for 10 minutes, then turn heat down to 160°C and continue roasting until chicken is done and the juices run clear. Remove chicken and leave to cool to room temperature.

- When cooled, peel and discard skin. Debone and shred by hand into fine strips. Reserve stuffing for the dressing.

- Combine chicken strips with jackfruit and all other ingredients including reserved stuffing. Season to taste with salt and pepper. Serve at room temperature with steamed rice.

Green Bean Salad with Chicken
Lawar Ayam Serves 4

This dish is always served during big religious or private celebrations and only the most senior and experienced men are allowed to mix the ingredients. Many traditional versions of this dish incorporate raw pounded meat and fresh blood in the dressing. As a variation to this recipe, use beef, pork, seafood, vegetables or young jackfruit in place of chicken.

Ingredients

Long beans	600 g, blanched and cut in 0.5-cm slices
Grated coconut	120 g, roasted
Garlic	6 cloves, peeled, sliced and fried
Shallots	6–8, peeled, sliced and fried
Large red chillies	2, seeded and cut into fine strips
Bird's eye chillies	4–6, finely sliced
Fried chilli dressing	3 tsp (see pg 39)
Spice paste for chicken	2 Tbsp (see pg 31)
Salt	1 tsp
Black peppercorns	2–3, crushed
Lime juice	1 tsp
Fried shallots	2 Tbsp (see pg 37)

Dressing

Minced chicken	250 g
Spice paste for chicken	2 Tbsp (see pg 31)
Banana leaf	1, cut into a 30-cm square
Aluminium foil	1 sheet, cut into a 35-cm square

Method

- Combine long beans, grated coconut, garlic, shallots, chillies, fried chilli dressing and spice paste in a large bowl. Mix well and set aside.

- Prepare dressing. Combine minced chicken with spice paste and mix well. Spoon minced chicken onto the centre of the banana leaf in a long line and roll up very tightly. Place banana leaf roll on aluminium foil and roll up again very tightly. Twist ends to tighten roll. Steam roll for 20 minutes then remove aluminium foil and banana leaf. Break chicken roll up with fork to get mince.

- Combine minced chicken with long bean mixture. Season to taste with salt, pepper and lime juice. Garnish with fried shallots.

Shredded Spiced Pork Salad

Be Celeng Mesitsit Serves 4

Ingredients

Pork topside	1 kg, cut into 4 steaks

Stock

Chicken or pork stock or water	5 litres (see pg 41)
Basic spice paste	125 g (see pg 30)
Lemon grass	2 stalks, bruised
***Salam* leaves**	4
Large red chillies	2
Kaffir lime leaves	3, bruised
Cloves	5, crushed
White peppercorns	1 tsp, crushed
Coriander seeds	1 Tbsp, crushed

Dressing

Basic spice paste	30 g (see pg 30)
Cloves	3, crushed
White peppercorns	2–3, ground
Salt	a pinch
Palm sugar	1 tsp, chopped
Cooking oil	2 Tbsp
Lime juice	2 Tbsp

Method

- Prepare stock. Combine stock ingredients and bring to the boil then simmer for 5 minutes. Add pork and boil for about 1$^1/_2$ hours until pork is very tender. (Meat must be so tender that the fibres separate very easily.) Leave to cool to room temperature in stock then drain. Reserve stock for future recipes. Pound to flatten meat and shred finely by hand.

- For the dressing, place all ingredients except cooking oil and lime juice into a food processor or stone mortar and grind into a very fine paste. Heat oil in heavy saucepan and sauté paste for 2 minutes over medium heat until fragrant.

- Add shredded pork, mix well and sauté until dry. Season with lime juice. Remove from heat and allow to cool. Serve at room temperature with steamed rice.

Note:

There are several methods to preparing this dish. As an alternative, cook as directed above, then after sautéing the meat, deep-fry in medium hot oil until crisp. Drain on a paper towel and store in an airtight container. This delicious dish is often eaten as a snack or served as an interesting topping on dishes. You may also replace pork with beef topside, basic spice paste with spice paste for beef (see pg 31) and chicken or pork stock with beef stock.

Starfruit Leaves with Minced Duckling
Don Jukut Blimbing Serves 4

If starfruit leaves are not available, use any type of spinach and cook using the same recipe.

Ingredients

Starfruit leaves	400 g, cleaned
Fried shallots	2 Tbsp (see pg 37)
Fried garlic	2 Tbsp (see pg 37)
Bird's eye chillies	2, sliced and fried until golden
Palm sugar	1 Tbsp, finely chopped
Lime juice	1 Tbsp
Grated coconut	4 Tbsp, lightly roasted
Salt	a pinch
Black peppercorns	2–3, crushed

Dressing

Cooking oil	1 Tbsp
Basic spice paste	20 g (see pg 30)
Duck giblets (or heart, liver, stomach)	200 g, finely minced
Duck or chicken stock	250 ml (see pg 41)
Coconut cream	250 ml

Method

- In stockpot, bring 3 litres of lightly salted water to the boil. Add starfruit leaves and bring back to the boil then simmer for 10 minutes. Drain leaves and cool in ice water. Drain again, dry well and slice evenly.

- Prepare dressing. Heat oil in a frying pan (skillet), add spice paste and sauté until fragrant. Add minced giblets and sauté until giblets change colour. Deglaze (see note below) with stock, mix well and bring back to simmer, then add coconut cream. Bring to the boil and simmer for 1 minute. Cool to room temperature.

- Mix in the starfruit leaves and dressing. Blend well and add all remaining ingredients. Mix well and season to taste with more salt and pepper as necessary.

- Garnish with crisp-fried duck skin as desired. To make, first blanch duck skin for 1 minute in boiling water. Then cool skin down to room temperature and pat dry. Slice evenly and fry the strips in hot oil until crisp.

Note:
To deglaze, put a small amount of stock in the pan and stir to loosen any browned bits of food.

Sate

Sate is a word that is regularly associated with Indonesian and Malaysian food. Most visitors to Bali will probably eat *sate* at their hotel or at a restaurant. But as with most kinds of Balinese food, the *sate* served at these establishments are different from traditional Balinese *sate*. Balinese *sate* are generally of two forms:

Sate Asem

This type of *sate* is made with chunks of meat threaded through a skewer. Whether pork or chicken, it is likely to be full of fat, skin and gristle. The meat is normally marinated for 15 minutes to 1 hour before skewering and grilling. Balinese *sate* is not usually served with any special sauce since the meat has already been marinated before cooking. However, a dip of light soy sauce and chopped bird's eye chilli is usually available for additional flavouring.

Sate Lembat or Sate Lilit

This is perhaps Bali's most original *sate*, made from pounded meat wrapped around a flattened skewer. This type of *sate* is time-consuming to make because of the care with which the meat must be prepared and then wrapped around the skewer. Only the choicest pork, chicken or duck meat is used, so it is not generally made except in connection with a religious ceremony, when lots of people are there to help and when large quantities of meat, spices and shredded coconut are available. For this reason, it is not usually available at *warungs* and tourists are not likely to encounter it except in the privacy of religious celebrations.

In Bali, *sate* is always grilled over coconut husks. Coconut husk does not burn satisfactorily unless fanned vigorously, and so grilling *sate* is a two-fisted job. The sticks of *sate* are held in the left hand while the fan is held in the right.

Bamboo *sate* sticks are normally used to thread the *sate* meat, but sometimes in the bigger markets, *sate* is threaded through the central stem of a coconut leaf. In former times in the southern part of Bali, two types of *sate* sticks were used. One was considered to be female: it had a broad tip and was used in the normal fashion for *sate lembat* or *sate lilit*. The other, called *gajih*, was considered to be male: it had a sharp tip upon which a small cube of meat was skewered.

Sate in Ceremonies

To the Balinese, everything is important in a ceremony. They would say, "all is necessary". And so, it is probably presumptuous for me to declare that *sate* is the most important of ceremonial foods. But so it seems to me, because if any part of the ceremony is to be used as a component of offerings, it is most likely to be the *sate*. And the size of a ceremony is always defined by the number of sticks of *sate* to be made. An ordinary ceremony would boast about 30 sticks of *sate* and enough other food to feed 10 people.

Minced Seafood *Sate*
Sate Lilit Ikan Serves 4

Ingredients

Snapper fillet	600 g, skinned and finely minced or chopped
Grated coconut	120 g
Coconut cream	45 ml
Spice paste for seafood	125 g (see pg 32)
Bird's eye chillies	3–5, very finely chopped
Kaffir lime leaves	5, finely chopped
Black peppercorns	2–3, finely crushed
Salt	a pinch
Palm sugar	1 Tbsp
Lemon grass or large bamboo skewers	

Method

- Combine all ingredients except lemon grass or bamboo skewers and mix into a very homogeneous sticky paste.

- Mould 1 heaped Tbsp of this mixture around the bulbous end of a lemon grass stalk or around a bamboo skewer. Continue until mixture is used up.

- Grill over very hot charcoal until golden brown. Serve with pickled vegetables (see pg 36).

Note:
It is extremely important to use only the freshest of fish. This recipe will not work with frozen fish as the mixture will become too watery and will not stick to the lemon grass or bamboo skewer.

Pork *Sate* with Liver
Sate Asam Celeng Serves 4

Ingredients

Coconut oil	1 Tbsp
Pork liver	400 g, sliced into 4 steaks
Pork tenderloin	400 g, cut into 1 x 0.5-cm cubes
Basic spice paste	125 g (see pg 30)
Bird's eye chillies	3–5, chopped
Palm sugar	2 Tbsp
Salt	a pinch

***Sate* skewers**

Method

- Heat oil in heavy frying pan (skillet). Fry liver steaks on both sides for 1 minute each side. Cool and slice into 1 x 0.5-cm cubes.

- Combine tenderloin, spice paste, chillies, palm sugar and salt. Mix well.

- Skewer 4–6 pieces of meat and liver very tightly on each *sate* skewer. Cover and leave to marinate in the refrigerator for 3 hours.

- Grill over very hot charcoal until golden brown. Serve with pickled vegetables (see pg 36).

Chicken *Sate*
Sate Ayam Serves 4

Ingredients

Chicken breast	750 g, cut into 1 x 0.75-cm strips
Bird's eye chillies	3–5, finely chopped
Palm sugar	2 Tbsp
Spice paste for chicken	125 g (see pg 31)
Salt	a pinch

***Sate* skewers**

Basting Mix

Spice paste for chicken	125 g (see pg 31)
Coconut oil	125 ml

Method

- Combine chicken, chillies, palm sugar, spice paste and salt and mix well.

- Skewer chicken with *sate* skewers, putting 4 strips tightly on each skewer. Cover and leave to marinate for 6 hours in the refrigerator.

- Meanwhile, prepare basting mix. Combine spice paste with coconut oil and mix well.

- Grill *sate* over very hot charcoal and baste frequently with basting mix until golden brown. Serve with pickled vegetables (see pg 36).

Note:
*To make **sate** with beef, lamb or pork, follow the directions as above but use spice paste for beef (see pg 31) if making beef **sate** and basic spice paste (see pg 30) if making pork and lamb **sate**.*

From top: Pork Sate *with Liver; Chicken* Sate

Minced Duck *Sate*
Sate Lembat Bebek Serves 4

Ingredients

Duck meat	400 g, minced
Pork neck or shoulder	200 g, minced
Basic spice paste	3 Tbsp (see page 30)
Bird's eye chillies	4, chopped
Yellow fried shallots	60 g (see pg 37)
Yellow fried garlic	40 g (see pg 37)
Palm sugar	1 tsp
Salt	a pinch
Black peppercorns	2–3, crushed
Grated coconut	120 g
Coconut cream	45 ml

Lemon grass or
   sate skewers

Method

- Combine all ingredients except lemon grass or *sate* skewers into a very homogeneous sticky paste.

- Mould 1 heaped Tbsp of this mixture around the bulbous end of a lemon grass stalk or around a *sate* skewer. Continue until mixture is used up.

- Grill over very hot charcoal until golden brown. Serve with pickled vegetables (see pg 36).

Note:
Sates *taste best when served still sizzling and hot from the grill. The Balinese enjoy their* sates *lightly burnt as this produces a distinct caramel flavour from the use of palm sugar.*

Snail *Sate*
Sate Kakul Serves 4

Ingredients

Canned snails	48, washed and drained
Basic spice paste	125 g (see pg 30)
Bird's eye chillies	2, finely chopped
Palm sugar	1 Tbsp, finely chopped
White peppercorns	2–3, crushed
Salt	to taste

Sate skewers

Sauce

Cooking oil	1 Tbsp
Basic spice paste	60 g (see pg 30)
Chicken stock	125 ml (see pg 41)
Coconut cream	125 ml
Kaffir lime leaves	2, chopped
Bird's eye chilli	1, chopped
Lemon grass	1 stalk, bruised

Method

- Combine snails, basic spice paste, chillies, palm sugar, pepper and salt and mix well. Skewer 4 snails very tightly on each *sate* skewer and leave to marinate for 1 hour. Place *sate* over very hot charcoal and grill until golden brown.

- For the sauce, place all ingredients except lemon grass in a food processor and purée very finely. Pour into a saucepan, add lemon grass and simmer until sauce thickens. Season to taste with salt and pepper if necessary. Serve warm with *sate*.

From top: Minced Duck Sate*; Snail* Sate

Soups

A standard soup at large Balinese feasts is the banana stem soup (*jukut ares*). A banana stem is boiled with spices and meat to make a rich stew. The stem of the young banana tree is considered the best for *ares*. In preparation for a feast, the stem is sliced thinly the evening before. Salt is added to the slices and they are left to sit until early the following morning. The mixture will then be kneaded to break up the stringy fibres and the salt flushed out by at least three washings in fresh water.

Chicken Soup with Vegetables and Eggs

Jukut Siap Serves 4

Ingredients

Chicken stock	3 litres (see pg 41)
Chicken spice paste	250 g (see pg 31)
Salam leaf	1
Kaffir lime leaves	2, bruised
Large red chillies	2
Bird's eye chillies	2, bruised
White peppercorns	2–3, crushed
Chicken	1, about 1.5 kg
White cabbage	200 g, finely shredded
Bean sprouts	200 g, cleaned
Celery	50 g, sliced
Spring onions (scallions)	50 g, finely sliced
Glass noodles (mung bean vermicelli)	100 g, blanched to cook
Salt	to taste
Hardboiled eggs	4, shelled and sliced
Fried shallots	2 Tbsp (see pg 37)

Method

- Bring stock to the boil, add spice paste, *salam* leaf, kaffir lime leaves, chillies and pepper and simmer for 5 minutes.

- Add chicken and simmer until chicken is very tender and meat almost falls off the bone. Lower heat and allow chicken to cool in stock. Remove chicken. Separate meat from bones and shred finely.

- Allow stock to simmer until reduced to about 1.5 litres, then add cabbage, bean sprouts, celery and spring onions and simmer for another 2 minutes.

- Add shredded chicken and glass noodles, and bring back to the boil then simmer for another 1 minute. Season to taste with salt. To serve, ladle soup into individual bowls and garnish with eggs and fried shallots.

Clear Chicken Soup

Gerangasem Siap Serves 4

This delicious soup is often prepared for ceremonies. The Balinese mix grated coconut with fresh chicken blood and squeeze it into the soup to give it a slightly creamy appearance. The soup is then ready and taken off the boil.

Ingredients

Cooking oil	1 Tbsp
Spice paste for chicken	125 g (see pg 31)
Minced chicken	300 g
Chicken heart, liver and stomach	200 g, minced (optional)
Chicken stock	1 litre (see pg 41)
Salam leaf	1
Lemon grass	1 stalk, bruised
Salt	a pinch
Ground black pepper	a pinch

Method

- Heat oil in heavy stockpot, add spice paste and sauté until fragrant. Add minced chicken and chicken parts. Continue to sauté until meat is evenly coloured.

- Add stock and all remaining ingredients. Simmer for 5 minutes. Season to taste with salt and pepper.

Note:
As a variation to this recipe, replace chicken with pork, duck or beef and change the spice paste accordingly.

Mushroom Soup
Wong Dadah Serves 4

Ingredients

Coconut oil	2 Tbsp
Spice paste for vegetables	200 g (see pg 30)
Black or shiitake mushrooms	250 g, washed and sliced
Chicken stock	625 ml (see pg 41)
Lemon grass	1 stalk, bruised
Kaffir lime leaves	2, bruised
Coconut cream	250 ml
Salt	a pinch
Ground black pepper	a pinch
Fried shallots	2 Tbsp (see pg 37)

Method

- Heat oil in heavy saucepan, add spice paste and sauté until fragrant. Add mushrooms and sauté for 2 more minutes.

- Pour in stock, add remaining ingredients except salt, pepper and fried shallots. Bring to the boil before lowering heat and simmering for 10 minutes. Season to taste with salt and pepper. Garnish with fried shallots.

Spinach and Tomato Cream Soup
Kuwah Bayem Tomat Serves 4

Ingredients

Spice paste for vegetables	200 g (see pg 30)
Cooking oil	2 Tbsp
Shallots	40 g, peeled and sliced
Garlic	20 g, peeled and sliced
Large red chillies	2, seeded and sliced
Vegetable or chicken stock	1 litre (see pg 41)
Coconut cream	250 ml
Salam leaves	2
Lemon grass	2 stalks, bruised
Spinach	400 g, blanched and cut
Tomatoes	4, peeled, seeded and sliced
Tamarind juice	3 Tbsp, from 3 Tbsp tamarind pulp soaked in 3 Tbsp warm water and strained
Salt	a pinch
White peppercorns	2–3, crushed

Method

- Place spice paste in a stone mortar or food processor and grind until very fine.

- Heat oil in saucepan, add shallots, garlic and chillies and sauté for 2 minutes. Add spice paste and continue to sauté until fragrant.

- Pour in stock and coconut cream. Add *salam* leaves and lemon grass and bring to the boil. Add spinach, tomatoes and tamarind juice. Bring to the boil and simmer for 5 minutes. Season to taste with salt and pepper.

From top: Mushroom Soup; Spinach and Tomato Cream Soup

Duck Soup with Banana Stems
Kuwah Ares Bebek Serves 4

The tender centre of young banana palms is used for this ceremonial dish in Bali. If banana stems are not available, replace with cabbage.

Ingredients

Young banana stem	600 g
Salt	6 Tbsp
Cooking oil	2 Tbsp
Basic spice paste	125 g (see pg 30)
Duck stock	1.5 litres (see pg 41)
Salam leaves	2
Lemon grass	1 stalk, bruised
Minced duck	300 g
Black peppercorns	1 pinch, crushed
Fried shallots	2 Tbsp (see pg 37)

Method

- Peel off hard outer layers of the banana stem and cut in half lengthwise. Place flat side on a chopping board and cut into thin slices. Place sliced banana stems into a deep bowl, sprinkle with salt and mix well for 5 minutes. This will break the fibres and release water from the stem. Rinse stems thoroughly under running water, then strain and dry well.

- Heat 1 Tbsp oil in a heavy stockpot, add four-fifths of the spice paste and sauté until fragrant. Add banana stem and continue to sauté for 2 minutes. Pour in stock, add *salam* leaves and lemon grass and bring to the boil. Leave to simmer until stems are tender. Set aside.

- In a saucepan, heat remaining oil, add remaining spice paste and sauté until fragrant. Add minced duck and continue to sauté until meat changes colour. Pour in banana stem soup and bring to the boil. Simmer for 5 more minutes. Season to taste with salt and pepper and garnish with fried shallots.

Note:
This dish is often prepared in a similar way with pork or chicken. If using pork, use basic spice paste and pork stock. If using chicken, use spice paste for chicken (see pg 31) and chicken stock.

Green Papaya Soup
Gedang Mekuah Serves 4

Ingredients

Green papaya	750 g
Vegetable or chicken stock	1 litre (see pg 41)
Spice paste for vegetables	125 g (see pg 30)
Salam leaves	2
Lemon grass	1 stalk, bruised
Crushed black peppercorns	a pinch
Salt	a pinch
Coconut cream	250 ml
Fried shallots	2 Tbsp (see pg 37)

Method

- Peel the papaya, cut in half lengthwise, scoop out and discard seeds. Slice the papaya lengthwise into 4–6 slices, then slice crosswise into 0.5-cm dices. Set aside.

- Heat stock, add spice paste, *salam* leaves, lemon grass, black pepper and salt and bring to the boil. Simmer for 2 minutes then add papaya and simmer gently until papaya is about 90 per cent tender.

- Add coconut cream and continue to simmer (do not boil) until papaya is completely tender. If the stock reduces too much, add more stock. Season to taste with salt and pepper. Garnish with fried shallots.

Note:
This delicious, creamy recipe can be easily adapted to suit various taste preferences. You can replace the spice paste for vegetables with spice paste for seafood (see pg 32) and garnish the dish with diced seafood of your choice.

Snail Soup with Spinach
Jukut Kakul Serves 4

Ingredients

Fresh snails	800 g or 36 canned snails, washed and drained
Cooking oil	1 Tbsp
Basic spice paste	125 g (see pg 30)
Chicken stock	1 litre (see pg 41)
Coconut cream	250 ml
Salam leaves	2
Salt	a pinch
Ground black pepper	a pinch
Spinach	200 g, cleaned, blanched and drained

Method

- If using fresh snails, wash thoroughly under running water. Bring 4 litres of lightly salted water to a fast boil then blanch snails for 20 seconds. Remove snails and cool in ice water. Drain. With a sharp knife, open the tip of the snail shell and clean out the intestines. Crack shells and remove snails. Wash snails thoroughly once again.

- In a saucepan, heat oil and sauté spice paste until fragrant. Stir in stock and coconut cream and add *salam* leaves, salt and pepper. Allow soup to simmer.

- Add snails, bring to the boil and simmer for 10 minutes. Finally add spinach and simmer soup for 1 more minute. Season to taste with salt and pepper.

Meats

The Balinese love meat. But for the average person, the price is prohibitive. Although a large number of animals wander around or are penned up in the average Balinese house yard, these animals are not used for food. This is because they are much more valuable when used for other purposes. Cows help to plough the fields. Pigs do not cost much to feed and they can be sold at the market when they are grown. Chickens lay eggs which are used for food and offerings. (The Balinese do not keep goats because they cause too much destruction, eating plants and flowers around the house.)

It would also not be practical for a single family or a small family group to butcher a large animal like a cow or pig as they would not be able to consume it entirely in one sitting. Most homes do not have refrigerators and so any animal that is killed for food must necessarily be a small one, since leftovers spoil very quickly without refrigeration.

Although over 90 per cent of the Balinese are Hindus, there is no religious precipitation against eating any kind of meat. Beef will, however, never be served at religious ceremonies and Hindu priests are forbidden to eat beef or pork.

Roast Suckling Pig
Guling Celeng

Ingredients

Suckling pig	1, about 6–8 kg, well-cleaned
Salt	1¹/₂ Tbsp
Cassava leaves	800 g, cleaned, blanched for 5 minutes and roughly cut
Shallots	200 g, peeled and sliced
Garlic	100 g, peeled and sliced
Ginger	100 g, peeled and chopped
Turmeric	350 g, peeled and chopped
Candlenuts	250 g, chopped
Galangal	100 g, peeled and finely chopped
Bird's eye chillies	120 g, sliced
Lemon grass	10 stalks, finely sliced
Coriander seeds	3 Tbsp, crushed
Black peppercorns	1 Tbsp, crushed
Dried prawn (shrimp) paste	1 Tbsp, roasted and crumbled
Kaffir lime leaves	5, finely chopped
Salam leaves	2
Turmeric water	250 ml (see pg 38)

Method

- Season inside and outside of suckling pig with salt.

- Combine all other ingredients, except turmeric water and mix thoroughly. Stuff suckling pig with mixture and close belly with string or a *sate* skewer. Brush the outside of the pig with turmeric water until the skin is shiny yellow.

- Place suckling pig on a roasting rack and roast in a preheated oven at 220°C for approximately 1 hour, then let it rest for 10 minutes in a warm place before serving.

- When serving, first remove the crisp skin with a carving knife, then loosen meat from the bones and cut into even dices or slices. Place 1 heaped Tbsp of stuffing on each serving plate and top with meat and skin.

Note:
If you have a large barbeque with a rotisserie or turning spit, you can cook the pig over a charcoal fire for an authentic Balinese flavour.

Braised Pork Knuckles

Kikil Celeng Mekuah Serves 4

Ingredients

Pork knuckles	1.2 kg, cut in 2.5-cm slices
Cooking oil	30 ml
Basic spice paste	250 g (see pg 30)
Lemon grass	2 stalks, bruised
Ginger	2.5-cm, peeled, sliced and bruised
Coriander seeds	1 tsp, crushed
Salam leaves	2
Large red chillies	3
Chicken stock	500 ml (see pg 41)
Salt	a pinch
Ground black pepper	a pinch

Garnish

Red chilli	1, sliced
Fried shallots (see pg 37)	
Lemon basil	

Method

- Bring 3 litres of lightly salted water to the boil in a stockpot. Add pork knuckles, reduce heat and simmer for about 45 minutes until meat is three-quarters cooked. Drain water and keep knuckles warm.

- Heat oil in deep heavy saucepan, add spice paste and sauté until fragrant. Add all other ingredients except chicken stock, salt, pepper and garnishes. Sauté for 2 minutes until spices change colour.

- Pour chicken stock into saucepan, mix well and bring to the boil. Add pork knuckles, mix well, and bring back to the boil, then reduce heat and simmer until knuckles are completely cooked. Should liquid reduce too much, add a little more chicken stock and let it boil again. Season with salt and pepper.

- Garnish with sliced red chilli, fried shallots and lemon basil.

Pork Braised in Coconut Milk
Nyanyat Celeng Serves 4

Ingredients

Coconut oil	2 Tbsp
Basic spice paste	250 g (see pg 30)
Pork shoulder or neck	800 g, cut in 2.5-cm cubes
Lemon grass	2 stalks, bruised
Salam leaves	3
Coriander seeds	1 Tbsp, crushed
Black peppercorn	1 Tbsp, crushed
Chicken stock	1 litre (see pg 41)
Coconut cream	250 ml
Salt	to taste
Fried shallots (see pg 37)	

Method

- Heat oil in heavy stewing pot and add spice paste. Sauté for 2 minutes until fragrant.

- Add pork cubes, lemon grass, *salam* leaves, coriander and pepper and continue to sauté until meat changes colour.

- Pour in enough stock to cover meat and bring to the boil. Simmer until meat is 90 per cent cooked. Continue to add more stock as liquid evaporates.

- Add coconut cream and bring back to the boil. Reduce heat and simmer until meat is tender and sauce thickens. Season to taste with salt and garnish with fried shallots.

Note:
This recipe can also be prepared with beef or lamb. If using lamb, add an additional 1 Tbsp crushed cardamom and 2 Tbsp rice vinegar. If using beef, use spice paste for beef (see pg 31) and add an additional 125 g of galangal, peeling, slicing and crushing it before use.

Tips for cooking stew
- Always use a proper stewing pot, which should never be covered.
- When pouring in liquid, do not add too much at one go. Allow the liquid to evaporate before adding more.
- Remember what grandma always did? Cook today and eat tomorrow.

Fried Pork Sausage

Urutan Celeng Serves 4

Ingredients

Pork shoulder or neck	500 g, roughly chopped
Pork fat	100 g, roughly chopped
Basic spice paste	125 g (see pg 30)
Tamarind pulp	2 Tbsp
Coriander seeds	1 tsp, finely crushed
Yellow fried shallots	2 Tbsp (see pg 37)
Yellow fried garlic	2 Tbsp (see pg 37)
Bird's eye chilli	1, finely chopped
Salt	a pinch
Black peppercorns	2, crushed
Pork intestine	1 m, thoroughly cleaned

Method

* Combine pork, pork fat, spice paste, tamarind pulp, coriander seeds, fried shallots, fried garlic and chilli and mix well into a smooth paste. Season to taste with salt and pepper.

* Tie one end of the pork intestine with string to seal it. Fit a large round nozzle into a pastry piping bag and fill with meat mixture. Place open end of intestine over nozzle and fill intestine tightly with meat mixture. Secure open end of intestine with string. Allow sausage to rest in a cool place for 2 hours.

* In a deep saucepan, bring 4 litres of water to the boil. Put sausage in and simmer over very low heat for 10 minutes. Drain water and dry sausage. Finally deep-fry or grill sausage until golden brown.

Braised Pork Ribs with Young Jackfruit

Balung Nangka Serves 4

Ingredients

Pork ribs	1 kg, cut in 3-cm pieces
Basic spice paste	250 g (see pg 30)
Cooking oil	2 Tbsp
Lemon grass	2 stalks, bruised
Salam leaves	4
Ginger	50 g, peeled, sliced and bruised
Large red chillies	2
Chicken stock	1.5 litres (see pg 41)
Young jackfruit	400 g, peeled, cleaned and cut into 2.5 x 1-cm pieces
Salt	to taste
Ground black pepper	to taste

Method

* Combine pork ribs with one-third of spice paste and mix well. Leave to marinate in a cool place for 1 hour.

* In a heavy stewing pot, heat oil, add remaining spice paste and sauté until fragrant.

* Add pork ribs, lemon grass, *salam* leaves, ginger and chillies and continue to sauté until pork ribs change colour. Add half of the chicken stock, bring to the boil and simmer until ribs are almost cooked. Gradually add more stock as it evaporates.

* In the meantime, cook young jackfruit. Bring 3 litres of lightly salted water to the boil, add jackfruit and simmer for about 15 minutes or until almost cooked. Drain and cool in ice water.

* Add jackfruit to stewing pot and simmer until ribs are tender. Season to taste with salt and pepper.

Pork in Sweet Soy Sauce

Be Celeng Base Manis Serves 4

Ingredients

Coconut oil	2 Tbsp
Shallots	70 g, peeled and sliced
Garlic	50 g, peeled and sliced
Pork shoulder or neck	800 g, cut in 2-cm cubes
Ginger	50 g, peeled and sliced
Sweet soy sauce	4 Tbsp
Light soy sauce	2 Tbsp
Black peppercorns	2–3, crushed
Chicken stock	1 litre (see pg 41)
Bird's eye chillies or large red chillies	6–10

Method

- Heat coconut oil in heavy saucepan. Add shallots and garlic and sauté for 2 minutes over medium heat or until lightly coloured.

- Add pork and ginger then continue to sauté for 2 more minutes over medium heat. Add sweet and light soy sauces and pepper. Continue to sauté for 1 more minute.

- Pour in half of the chicken stock, add chillies and simmer over medium heat for approximately 1 hour. Gradually add more stock as liquid evaporates. When cooked, there should be very little sauce left and the meat should be shiny and dark brown in colour.

Note:

Keep liquid to an absolute minimum and do not cover the saucepan during the cooking process. This will guarantee a lovely dark brown stew with a shiny sauce.

Ox Tongue in Sweet Nutmeg Sauce

Semur Lidah Serves 4

Ingredients

Beef stock	2.5 litres (see pg 41)
Spice paste for beef	250 g (see pg 31)
Salam leaves	4
Ground black pepper	1/2 tsp
Ground nutmeg	1/4 tsp
Kaffir lime leaves	4
Ox tongue	600 g
Sweet soy sauce	4 Tbsp
Potatoes	3, medium, peeled and cut into 2-cm cubes
Salt	to taste
Ground black pepper	a pinch

Method

- In a heavy stockpot, pour in beef stock. Add spice paste, *salam* leaves, pepper, nutmeg and kaffir lime leaves and bring to the boil. Lower heat and simmer for 2 minutes.

- Add ox tongue, bring back to the boil and simmer over very low heat until tongue is cooked and very tender. This will take approximately 3 hours.

- Remove cooked ox tongue from stockpot and plunge into ice water and cool. Peel skin off with the help of a sharp knife. Slice ox tongue into thin, even slices and set aside.

- Strain stock in stockpot into another saucepan. Stir in sweet soy sauce and add potatoes. Simmer until potatoes are tender.

- Add ox tongue and bring back to simmer. Season to taste with salt and pepper.

Dry-fried Beef
Be Abon

Ingredients

Beef or chicken stock or water	5 litres (see pg 41)
Spice paste for beef	200 g (see pg 31)
Lemon grass	2 stalks, bruised
Salam leaves	4
Large red chillies	2
Galangal	80 g, peeled, sliced and bruised
Cloves	5
Black peppercorns	1/2 Tbsp, crushed
Coriander seeds	1/2 Tbsp, crushed
Beef topside	1 kg, cut into 4 steaks

Dressing

Spice paste for beef	125 g (see pg 31)
Cloves	3, crushed
Black peppercorns	2–3, crushed
Palm sugar	1/2 Tbsp, chopped
Cooking oil	2 Tbsp
Lime juice	2 Tbsp
Salt	a pinch
Ground black pepper	a pinch

Method

- In a deep stockpot, bring stock and all the ingredients, except beef and dressing ingredients, to the boil and simmer for 5 minutes.

- Add beef and boil for approximately 1 1/2 hours until beef is very tender. Leave beef to cool to room temperature in stock, then remove and dry well. Beef must be so tender that its fibres separate very easily. Reserve stock for use in other recipes.

- Slice beef into even slices or pound until flat and shred by hand into fine fibres. Set aside.

- For the dressing, place all ingredients except oil, lime juice, salt and pepper into a food processor or stone mortar and grind into a very fine paste.

- Heat oil in heavy saucepan and sauté paste for 2 minutes over medium heat until fragrant. Add shredded beef, mix well and sauté until dry. Season with lime juice, salt and pepper, then leave to cool and drain before storing in an airtight container. Use as a side dish or as a garnish.

- Alternatively marinate sliced or shredded beef with the dressing for 1 hour then season with lime juice, salt and pepper. Fry in medium hot oil until very crisp. Drain on paper towels, cool and store in an airtight container. Use as a side dish or as a garnish.

Note:
Chicken can be prepared the same way, except that the meat is simply cut into pieces and not pounded or shredded.

Braised Beef in Coconut Milk
Be Sampi Membase Bali Serves 4

Ingredients

Coconut oil	2 Tbsp
Spice paste for beef	250 g (see pg 31)
Beef topside	800 g, cut in 2.5-cm cubes
Lemon grass	2 stalks, bruised
Salam leaves	2
Galangal	70 g, peeled, sliced and bruised
Beef or chicken stock	1 litre (see pg 41)
Coconut cream	1 litre
Salt	to taste
Ground black pepper	to taste
Fried shallots (see pg 37)	

Method

- Heat oil in a heavy saucepan or stewing pot. Add spice paste and fry over low heat for 2 minutes or until fragrant.

- Add beef cubes, lemon grass, *salam* leaves and galangal and sauté for 2 more minutes. Add half of the stock and bring to the boil. Reduce heat and simmer until meat is 90 per cent cooked. Continue to add more stock as it evaporates.

- Add coconut cream, bring back to the boil and simmer until meat is tender and sauce has thickened. Season to taste with salt and pepper. Garnish with fried shallots.

Balinese Lamb Stew

Kambing Mekuah Serves 4

Ingredients

Cooking oil	2 Tbsp
Basic spice paste	250 g (see pg 30)
Coriander seeds	1 Tbsp, crushed
Boneless lamb leg or shoulder	800 g, cut in 2-cm cubes
Cardamom pods	12, bruised and ground
Lemon grass	1 stalk, bruised
Chicken stock	1 litre (see pg 41)
White vinegar	1 Tbsp
Coconut cream	250 ml

Method

- Heat oil in heavy saucepan. Add spice paste and coriander seeds and sauté for 2 minutes over medium heat.

- Add lamb, cardamom and lemon grass and continue to sauté until lamb changes colour.

- Add 375 ml chicken stock and vinegar and bring to the boil, then simmer until lamb is about 90 per cent cooked. Add more stock as it evaporates.

- Finally add coconut cream and bring to the boil. Reduce heat to very low and simmer until lamb is tender. Add more chicken stock as necessary. The sauce should be creamy in consistency.

Poultry

The Balinese distinguish between two types of chicken: the *siap kampong*, chickens of the home yard, and the *siap* Java, where Java does not really refer to the island of Java, but, rather, any place outside of Bali. (The Balinese divide the world into two parts, Bali, and everything else—Java.) The *siap kampong* are free range chickens, left to roam the yards and eat whatever they find. *Siap* Java are chickens raised in enclosures with special feeds.

Curiously enough, the *siap kampong*, the scrawny, wiry local chicken commands a much higher price then the fat *siap* Java, and Balinese people prefer to eat the former.

Ducks commonly reside in areas where there are irrigated rice fields. Farmers generally raise ducks for their eggs rather then their meat. In parts of Bali where there are no irrigated fields, one almost never sees ducks—not in the fields nor in the markets, although duck eggs are available and sold in almost every market.

Among the Balinese, it is generally felt that the duck is an inherently more intelligent animal than the chicken, since chickens run around meaninglessly, eating whatever they find, whereas ducks stick together, are rather particular about what they eat, and are able to exist happily on water or on land. This sentiment inevitably leads the Balinese to prefer duck meat to chicken meat, although it is not commonly available to the average Balinese family.

Chicken in Spiced Coconut Sauce

Be Siap Base Kalas Serves 4

Ingredients

Coconut oil	1 Tbsp
Spice paste for chicken	250 g (see pg 31)
Lemon grass	1 stalk, bruised
Salam leaf	1
Kaffir lime leaf	1, torn
Chicken thighs	800 g, deboned and cut into 2.5-cm cubes
Salt	a pinch
White peppercorns	2–3, crushed
Chicken stock	250 ml (see pg 41)
Coconut cream	250 ml

Method

- Heat oil in heavy saucepan. Add spice paste and sauté for 2 minutes over low heat until fragrant. Add lemon grass, *salam* leaf, kaffir lime leaf and chicken and continue to sauté for another 2 minutes. Season with salt and pepper.

- Pour in chicken stock, bring to the boil and simmer for 1 minute. Add coconut cream, bring back to the boil and simmer over very low heat until chicken is cooked and sauce thickens.

Note:

Always keep the sauce light in consistency to prevent it from curdling. If the sauce becomes too thick, stir in some chicken stock.

Grilled Chicken
Siap Mepanggang Serves 4

Ingredients

Spring chickens	4, each about 800 g
Cooking oil	2 Tbsp
Spice paste for chicken	250 g (see pg 31)
Lemon grass	2 stalks, bruised
Salam leaves	3
Bird's eye chillies	3–4, bruised (optional)
Chicken stock	1 litre (see pg 41)
Coconut cream	250 ml
Salt	a pinch
Black peppercorns	2–3, crushed

Basting Mix

Spice paste for chicken	10 g (see pg 31)
Cooking oil	125 ml

Method

- Cut along the backbone of the spring chickens, open butterfly style and flatten. Set aside.

- Heat oil in a heavy saucepan, add spice paste and sauté for 2 minutes.

- Add all other ingredients except chickens and basting mix and bring to the boil. Add chickens, lower heat and simmer until three-quarters cooked, taking care to turn chickens around frequently. Remove from heat and cool chickens to room temperature.

- Meanwhile, prepare basting mix. Combine ingredients and mix well. Set aside.

- When chickens are cool, drain from sauce and dry well. Reserve sauce.

- Grill chickens over very hot glowing charcoal until golden brown. Baste with basting mix frequently on both sides to prevent chickens from burning.

- Bring reserved sauce back to simmer and allow to reduce until all liquid has evaporated. Serve as a dipping sauce for the chicken.

- Serve chicken with pickled vegetables (see pg 36).

Tip: To prepare Balinese Fried Chicken (*Siap Megoreng*), follow the steps described above, but instead of grilling the chicken over charcoal, fry in medium hot oil until golden brown.

Crispy Fried Duck

Calokok Bebek Serves 4

About 80 per cent of all food cooked in Bali is fried. This is one such dish.

Ingredients

Duck	1, about 2 kg, cleaned and cut into 8 pieces
Basic spice paste	250 g (see pg 30)
Cooking oil	2 Tbsp
Lemon grass	2 stalks, bruised
Cinnamon stick	5-cm length
Salam leaf	1
Chicken or duck stock	2 litres (see pg 41)

Marinade

Basic spice paste	125 g (see pg 30)
Salt	a pinch
Black peppercorns	2–3, crushed
Rice flour	150 g

Method

- Marinate duck with half the basic spice paste for 1 hour in a cool place.

- Heat oil in a heavy saucepan, add remaining spice paste, lemon grass, cinnamon stick and *salam* leaf and sauté for 2 minutes. Pour in stock, bring to the boil and simmer for 1 minute.

- Add duck and bring back to the boil then simmer for 30–40 minutes until duck is 80 per cent cooked. Remove from heat and leave duck to cool in the stock. When cooled, remove from stock and drain well.

- Marinate duck. Rub duck with spice paste, salt and pepper and dust evenly with rice flour. Deep-fry in medium hot oil until duck is crisp and golden brown in colour. Drain well before serving.

Duck Curry

Bebek Menyanyat Serves 4

Ducks waddling in the rice fields or following after a flag held by their owner (or the owner's children) are a common sight in Bali. On festive occasions, duck is a favourite dish. Spiced stuffed duck baked in banana leaf is popular, as is this curry-like dish. Use chicken in place of duck if preferred.

Ingredients

Duck	1, about 2 kg, cleaned and cut into 12 pieces
Basic spice paste	400 g (see pg 30)
Cooking oil	2 Tbsp
Duck or chicken stock	1 litre (see pg 41)
Coconut cream	250 ml
Black peppercorns	1 tsp, crushed
Salt	to taste

Method

- Mix duck well with one-third of the spice paste and refrigerate or leave in a cool place to marinate for 1 hour.

- Heat oil in a heavy stewing pot, add remaining spice paste and sauté until fragrant.

- Add duck and continue to sauté until meat changes colour.

- Add half the stock or just enough to cover duck pieces. Bring to the boil, reduce heat and simmer until duck is cooked. Check liquid level regularly and add more stock as necessary.

- Continue until duck is tender. Add coconut milk and allow sauce to reduce to a creamy consistency. Season to taste with salt and pepper.

Seafood

Fish is a major source of food for almost all Balinese people and especially for those who live on or near the sea. This is because fish is relatively cheap, not difficult to catch and readily available in all markets. Fishing is one of the principal occupations of most Balinese who live along the coast, or at least until the advent of mass tourism that shifted the economy. Fish can be cheaply preserved temporarily by boiling in salted water, or more or less permanently by salting, or simply by drying, and since none of these methods requires much expense or equipment, preserved or dried fish is available at affordable prices far below that of meat in almost all villages. And unlike other sources of meat such as pigs or cows, fish is favoured also because it comes in smaller portions, making it easy for an average family to consume it without wastage.

While fresh poultry and meat are available in the village markets inland, fresh fish is usually in limited supply because of the difficulty involved in transportation, since refrigerated trucks and frozen fish are not part of the Balinese tradition. If fish is to be sold at some distance from the coast, it is often salted, boiled in brine or dried. Seasonal fresh fish is however available in Denpasar and they are usually sold within half a day of being caught so there is no need for preservation.

While we might imagine that the families of fishermen enjoy eating an abundance of seafood, this is far from the truth. In Bali, if a person can sell an item that was caught or cultivated, it would be sold and the money would be used to purchase cheaper items of food or daily necessities.

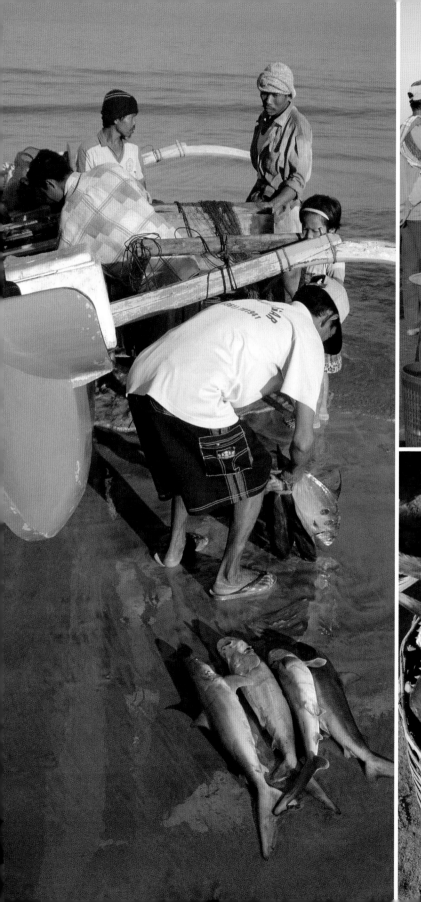

A Natural Fish Trap

Jimbaran Bay is a large natural fish trap, formed by the converging east coast of Java and west coast of Bali. This inverted funnel shape of the strait traps the rich marine life from the Indian Ocean, contributing to the livelihood of a good many people who live along Bali's southwest coast or East Java.

Fish Head Soup

Sop Kepala Ikan Serves 4

Ingredients

Seafood or chicken stock	1 litre (see pg 41)
Spice paste for seafood	125 g (see pg 32)
Salam leaves	3
Kaffir lime leaves	2, bruised
Bilimbi	4, bruised
Fish heads	4, each about 250 g, cleaned and cut into half lengthwise
Tomatoes	4, peeled, seeded and sliced
Salt	a pinch
Ground black pepper	a pinch

Method

- Combine stock, spice paste, *salam* leaves, kaffir lime leaves and bilimbi. Allow to simmer for 2 minutes.

- Add fish heads and continue to simmer until fish is almost cooked. Add tomatoes and simmer for 1 more minute. Season to taste with salt and pepper.

Note:
Have your fishmonger cut the fish heads well behind the gills so there will be more meat.

Fried Seafood Cake Serves 4

Ingredients

Snapper or any firm fish fillet	600 g, skinned and finely minced
Spice paste for seafood	125 g (see pg 32)
Grated coconut	90 g, roasted
Coconut cream	125 ml
Bird's eye chillies	3–5, finely chopped
Kaffir lime leaves	3, finely chopped
Palm sugar	1 Tbsp, chopped
White peppercorns	2–3, crushed
Salt	a pinch

Method

- Combine all ingredients and mix into a very homogeneous sticky paste.

- Mould 1 heaped Tbsp of mixture into an even cake. Continue until mixture is used up. Deep-fry or pan-fry until golden brown. Drain well.

Note:
There are several ways to use this delicious seafood mix. You can mould it into cakes as above then coat with grated or desiccated coconut and pan-fry until golden brown. Another way is to steam it wrapped in banana leaf. Spoon 2 Tbsp of the mixture onto a banana leaf, top with 2 slices of tomatoes and a sprig of lemon basil. Fold the long edges of the banana leaf in towards each other to enclose the filling. Secure the open ends with bamboo skewers then steam the parcels for 7–10 minutes.

Marinated Grilled Fish

Be Pasih Mepanggang Serves 4

Ingredients

Whole fish (snapper, travelly, mackerel, etc.)	1, about 1 kg, cleaned , or 1 kg assorted seafood (fish fillets, prawns (shrimps), clams, mussels etc.)
Salt	1 tsp
Ground white pepper	1 tsp
Lime juice	2 Tbsp
Spice paste for seafood	200 g (see pg 32)
Cooking oil	

Grilling Paste

Seafood spice paste	125 g
Vegetable oil	125 ml

Method

- If using whole fish, cut it in half, using a sharp knife, butterfly style, starting from the head down towards the tail. Then, make 4 slits about 1-cm deep on the side of fish where the bones are. (This will allow the seasoning to penetrate the fish and the fish will also cook more evenly.)

- Rub outside of whole fish with remaining marinade. If possible, leave the fish to marinate for several hours to improve the flavour.

- If using assorted seafood, marinate with salt, pepper, lime juice and spice paste.

- Combine ingredients for grilling paste and mix well. Brush a little paste over whole fish or assorted seafood.

- Place whole fish or assorted seafood on a charcoal grill and cook over medium heat. Turn fish over frequently and brush with grilling paste each time. This will prevent the fish from drying out and the spices from burning.

- Serve with spiced tomato sauce (see pg 32), shallot and lemon grass dressing (see pg 40) and steamed white rice.

Note:

When selecting fresh fish, there are several aspects to look out for. The eyes should be crystal bright and clear, and stick out in a round shape from the eye socket. The fish has to look alive, and the flesh should be firm and still have its natural slime on. The fish must also be free of any odours.

Prawns in Spiced Tomato Sauce
Sambel Udang Serves 4

Ingredients

Cooking oil	1 Tbsp
Large prawns (shrimps)	350 g, cleaned and deveined
Spice paste for seafood	60 g (see pg 32)
Spiced tomato sauce	1 Tbsp (see pg 32)
Lemon grass	1 stalk, bruised
Kaffir lime leaves	2, bruised
Bird's eye chilli	1 (optional)
Salt	a pinch
Black peppercorns	2–3, crushed
Chicken stock	125 ml (see pg 41)
Coconut cream	250 ml
Bilimbi	1, crushed
Tomato	1, peeled, seeded and cut into wedges
Lime juice	1 Tbsp
Fried shallots (see pg 37)	

Method

- Heat oil in saucepan. Add prawns and sauté on both sides until colour changes.

- Add spice paste, spiced tomato sauce, lemon grass, kaffir lime leaves, chilli, salt and pepper. Mix well and continue to sauté for 1 more minute.

- Add stock and coconut cream and bring to the boil. Reduce heat, add bilimbi and tomato wedges and simmer for another 1 minute. Should sauce thicken too much, add more stock as necessary.

- Season with lime juice and garnish with fried shallots.

Squid with Green Papayas
Penyon Kenus Serves 4

Ingredients

Squid	800 g
Spice paste for seafood	125 g (see pg 32)
Lime juice	2 Tbsp
Salt	a pinch
Ground white pepper	a pinch
Cooking oil	3 Tbsp
Shallots	50 g, peeled and sliced
Large red chillies	2, seeded and sliced
Lemon grass	2 stalks, bruised
Kaffir lime leaves	2, bruised
Chicken stock	375 ml (see pg 41)
Green papaya	400 g, peeled, seeded, sliced and blanched

Method

- Clean squid. Peel off skin and remove tentacles and head. Slice open squid tube lengthwise and wash thoroughly. Slice into even strips.

- Marinate squid with one-third of the spice paste, lime juice, salt and pepper for 10 minutes.

- Heat 1 Tbsp oil in a frying pan (skillet), add squid and sear over high heat for 1 minute on each side. Set aside and keep warm.

- In another pan, heat 1 Tbsp oil, add shallots and chillies and sauté for 2 minutes. Add remaining spice paste, lemon grass and kaffir lime leaves and continue to sauté until fragrant.

- Pour in stock, bring to the boil and simmer for 1 minute. Add squid and green papaya. Bring to the boil and simmer for 30 seconds. Season to taste with salt and pepper.

Assorted Seafood Braised in Coconut Milk
Hasil Laut Bumbu Kuning Serves 4

Ingredients

Coconut oil	1 tsp
Spice paste for seafood	125 g (see pg 32)
Lemon grass	1 stalk, bruised
Kaffir lime leaves	2
Bird's eye chillies	3
Assorted seafood (fish fillet, squid, crab, mussels, scallops etc.)	600 g, cleaned
Chicken stock	125 ml (see pg 41)
Coconut cream	250 ml
Salt	a pinch
Black peppercorns	2–3, crushed

Method

- Heat oil in heavy saucepan. Add spice paste, lemon grass, kaffir lime leaves and chillies. Sauté over medium heat for 2 minutes.

- Add seafood and sauté for 3 minutes. Pour in chicken stock and bring to the boil. Reduce heat and simmer for 1 minute then pour in coconut cream and bring back to the boil. Simmer for another minute and season to taste with salt and pepper.

Banana Leaf Cooking

The banana leaf is the original disposable, plate and food wrapper of Asia. Food stalls sell their dishes and snacks on banana leaf plates or wrapped in a banana leaves for takeaways. In Bali, banana leaves are folded in specific ways for specific purposes, and, of course, a vocabulary exists to refer to each way. A cake that is wrapped in one way has an entirely different name if it is wrapped in another way. Food must also be wrapped in an appropriate manner. For example, if you buy *nasi campur* to take away, it will be wrapped in a particular way with the folds of the leaf skewered with slivers of bamboo. But if you buy several sticks of grilled *sate* to take away, they will be wrapped in an entirely different fashion. In fact, the contents of banana leaf packages can be determined by simply noting how they are wrapped.

Many Balinese foods are also boiled or steamed in banana leaves in order to keep the contents together, such as with rice cakes. My favourite banana leaf wrapped food is *sumping*, a dough made from sticky rice flour, with a slice of banana, rolled up in a banana leaf and steamed in a rice cooker.

If one lives in a rural village, banana leaves are easily obtainable fresh and free straight from the trees. In the less rural areas, banana leaves can be easily purchased from the village market. Banana leaves must be used within a day or two after it is cut from the plant or it becomes brown and brittle. Because of this, banana leaves are usually not cut, but left on the plant to dry up slowly and naturally. They are then cut off the plant and will remain supple and strong more or less indefinitely. This naturally dried leaf is more flexible than fresh banana leaves and tears less readily, making it the preferred medium for making very small food containers, such as for offerings.

Other types of leaves used to wrap and package food are coconut leaves and bamboo leaves. The pale, immature coconut leaves are commonly used for making offerings, while the mature green leaves are used for making various food containers. Bamboo leaves are traditionally used to wrap Balinese cakes but these cakes are only made on rare occasions.

Tum

*Tum, leaf-wrapped bundles of highly seasoned food, are made
with almost any basic ingredient, ranging from eels,
to chicken, duck, pork and beef.*

Grilled Fish in Banana Leaf
Pesan Be Pasih Makes 14

*If banana leaves are not available, use corn husks. You may also
use greaseproof paper or aluminium foil although they   are not
ideal in terms of flavour.*

Ingredients

Fish fillet	**600 g, skinned and cut into 1.5-cm dices**
Salt	**a pinch**
White peppercorns	**2–3, crushed**
Spice paste for seafood	**125 g (see pg 32)**
Tomatoes	**2, each cut into 14 slices**
Lemon basil	**2 sprigs**
***Salam* leaves**	**14**
Banana leaves	**8, each cut into two 15-cm squares**
Bamboo skewers	

Method

- Season fish with salt and pepper and coat evenly with spice paste.

- Place a *salam* leaf in the centre of a banana leaf. Top with 1 Tbsp of marinated fish, 2 slices of tomato and lemon basil leaves. Fold long edges of banana leaf in towards each other to enclose filling. Secure open ends with bamboo skewers. Continue until ingredients are used up.

- Cover parcels and leave to marinate in a cool place for 30 minutes before cooking.

- There are a number of ways to cook these tasty parcels:
  - Steam for 7 minutes.
  - Steam for 4 minutes then place on a charcoal grill and cook for 3 more minutes until banana leaves are evenly browned.
  - Grill over very low heat for about 9 minutes.
  - Roast in a preheated oven at 180°C for 9 minutes.
  - The most common way to cook these parcels in Bali is to place them on a hot iron plate or frying pan (skillet) without oil and grill until done.

Note:
*It is important not to overcook these delicate parcels as the fish will
dry out very easily. Instead, undercook them slightly and leave in a
warm place for 5 minutes before serving.*

Diced Mackerel in Banana Leaf

Tambusan Be Pasih Makes 14

This spicy fish dish is excellent for barbeques. The Balinese often prepare catfish or any other type of freshwater fish in this way.

Ingredients

Mackerel fillets	600 g, skinned and cut into 2.5-cm cubes
Spice paste for seafood	125 g (see pg 32)
Tamarind juice	3 Tbsp, from 3 Tbsp tamarind pulp soaked in 3 Tbsp warm water and strained
Black peppercorns	2–3, crushed
Salt	a pinch
Kaffir lime leaves	3, rolled up and finely cut
Cooking oil	3 Tbsp
Lemon basil	2 sprigs
Salam leaves	14
Banana leaves	7, each cut into two 20-cm squares
Bamboo skewers	

Method

- In deep bowl, combine mackerel cubes, spice paste, tamarind juice, pepper, salt, kaffir lime leaves and oil, and mix well. Cover and leave to marinate in a cool place for 2 hours.

- Place a *salam* leaf in the centre of a banana leaf square. Top with 2 heaped Tbsp of mackerel mixture and a lemon basil leaf. Fold long edges of banana leaf in towards each other to enclose filling. Secure open ends with bamboo skewers. Continue until ingredients are used up.

- Place parcels directly onto moderately hot charcoal and roast for 1 hour. Alternatively, bake on a rack in a preheated oven at 180°C, or under a grill for about 30 minutes.

- Serve with shallot and lemon grass dressing (see pg 40), spiced tomato sauce (see pg 32), wedges of lime and steamed rice.

Minced Eel in Banana Leaf

Lumrah Lindung Makes 20

Ingredients

Eel	800 g, cut into 50 g dices
Salt	a pinch
Black peppercorns	2–3, crushed
Basic spice paste	125 g (see pg 30)
Cooking oil	4 Tbsp
Shallot and lemon grass dressing	3 Tbsp (see pg 40)
Bird's eye chillies	2, chopped
Palm sugar	1/2 Tbsp, chopped
Salam leaves	20
Banana leaves	10, each cut into two 20-cm squares
Bamboo skewers	

Method

- Season eel with salt and pepper and marinate with a quarter of the spice paste.

- Heat oil, add eel and sauté until about 80 per cent done. Drain oil and leave eel to cool.

- Place cooled eel into a food processor or stone mortar and grind roughly. Remove and mix well with shallot and lemon grass dressing, chillies and palm sugar. Season to taste with salt and pepper.

- Place a *salam* leaf in the centre of each banana leaf square and spoon 2 heaped Tbsp mixture on top. Fold long edges of banana leaf in towards each other to enclose filling. Secure open ends with bamboo skewers. Continue until ingredients are used up. Steam parcels for 7 minutes.

From top: Diced Mackerel in Banana Leaf ; Minced Eel in Banana Leaf

Steamed Prawns in Banana Leaf

Palem Udang Makes 20

Ingredients

Prawns (shrimps)	800 g, peeled, cleaned and diced
Spice paste for seafood	125 g (see pg 32)
Grated coconut	90 g
Coconut cream	125 ml
Yellow fried shallots	2 Tbsp (see pg 37)
Yellow fried garlic	2 Tbsp (see pg 37)
Bird's eye chillies	2, chopped
Palm sugar	$^1/_2$ Tbsp, chopped
Kaffir lime leaves	2, finely chopped
Lime juice	1 Tbsp
Salt	a pinch
White peppercorns	2–3, crushed
Banana leaves	10, each cut into two 20-cm squares
Bamboo skewers	

Method

- Combine all ingredients except banana leaves and bamboo skewers and mix well. Cover and leave to marinate in a cool place for 1 hour.

- Spoon 2 heaped Tbsp of mixture onto to a banana leaf and fold long edges of banana leaf in towards each other to enclose filling. Secure open ends with bamboo skewers. Continue until ingredients are used up. Steam for 7 minutes.

Note:
You can adapt this recipe to make Steamed Crab in Banana Leaf (Palem Yuyu). Simply replace prawns (shrimps) with crab meat.

Steamed Mushrooms in Banana Leaf

Pesan Wong Serves 4

Ingredients

Coconut oil	2 Tbsp
Large red chillies	3, seeded and sliced
Bird's eye chillies	2, sliced
Dried prawn (shrimp) paste	1 tsp, roasted
Salt	a pinch
Shiitake mushrooms	250 g, cleaned and diced
Banana leaf	1, cut into a 15 x 18-cm sheet
Bamboo skewers	

Method

- Combine coconut oil, chillies, dried prawn paste and salt in a food processor or stone mortar and grind into a fine paste.

- Mix mushrooms in with paste, allowing paste to coat mushrooms well.

- Place mushroom mixture in the centre of the banana leaf and fold long edges of banana leaf in towards each other to enclose filling. Secure open ends with bamboo skewers. Steam or grill parcel for about 10 minutes. (You may also make many small parcels as shown on the right instead of a big one.)

Diced Chicken in Banana Leaf
Pesan Ayam Makes 16

Ingredients

Boneless chicken leg	800 g, diced
Spice paste for chicken	125 g (see pg 31)
Grated coconut	90 g, roasted
Coconut cream	125 ml
Fried chilli dressing	3 Tbsp (see pg 39)
Palm sugar	1 Tbsp, chopped
Kaffir lime leaves	2–3, finely chopped
Lime juice	$1/2$ Tbsp
Salt	a pinch
White peppercorns	2–3, crushed
Salam leaves	16
Banana leaves	8, each cut into 20-cm squares
Bamboo skewers	

Method

- Combine all ingredients except *salam* leaves, banana leaves and bamboo skewers and mix well. Cover and leave to marinate in a cool place for 1 hour.

- Place a *salam* leaf in the centre of a banana leaf and spoon 2 heaped Tbsp of the filling on top. Fold long edges of banana leaf in towards each other to enclose filling. Secure open ends with bamboo skewers. Continue until ingredients are used up.

- Grill under very low heat for approximately 7 minutes until well cooked.

Minced Duck in Banana Leaf

Tum Bebek Makes 12

Ingredients

Duck	600 g, deboned, skinned and minced
Basic spice paste	3 Tbsp (see pg 30)
Bird's eye chillies	4, chopped
Palm sugar	1 tsp, chopped
Coconut cream	80 ml
Coconut oil	3 Tbsp
Shallots	60 g, peeled and sliced
Garlic	40 g, peeled and sliced
Turmeric	20 g, peeled and finely sliced
Salt	a pinch
Black peppercorns	2–3, crushed
Salam leaves	12
Banana leaves	6, each cut into two 20-cm squares + a few extra strips
Bamboo skewers	

Method

- Combine minced duck, spice paste, chillies, palm sugar and coconut cream and mix well.

- Heat oil in a frying pan (skillet). Add shallots, garlic and turmeric and sauté until lightly browned. Cool and fold into duck mixture. Season to taste with salt and pepper.

- Place a *salam* leaf in the centre of a banana leaf. Top with 1 Tbsp of mixture and enclose by folding the banana leaf into a little 'purse'. Finish by wrapping over with an extra strip of banana leaf. Secure with a bamboo skewer. Continue until ingredients are used up. Steam parcels for about 10 minutes until well cooked.

Note:

This mixture can also be used for duck sate. Simply replace the coconut cream with 150 g grated coconut. Mould 1 heaped Tbsp of the mixture around a large bamboo skewer or around the bulbous end of a stalk of lemon grass. Continue until the mixture is used up. Grill sate over a charcoal fire until golden brown.

Roast Duck in Banana Leaf

Bebek Betutu Serves 4

In the past 13 years that I have stayed in Bali, there was only once where I had the pleasure of witnessing this tasty duck dish prepared and cooked the traditional way. This took place in a private home just outside the artists' village of Ubud, in central Bali. There, the duck was not wrapped in banana leaves but in sheets of sliced banana stem. This completely seals the duck from the burning charcoal in which the duck is buried. As a result, the duck will not burn, but will be steamed to perfection in the heat. Today, banana leaves are used to simplify the preparation. In the photograph, I have done it the traditional Balinese way with sheets of banana stem.

Ingredients

Duck	1, about 2 kg, cleaned
Salt	a pinch
Black peppercorns	1 tsp, crushed
Shallots	50 g, peeled and sliced
Garlic	25 g, peeled and chopped
Ginger	25 g, peeled and chopped
Turmeric	90 g, peeled and chopped
Candlenuts	60 g, chopped
Galangal	25 g, peeled and chopped
Bird's eye chillies	30 g, finely sliced
Lemon grass	4 stalks, bruised, finely sliced and chopped
Lesser galangal	25 g, cleaned and chopped
Dried prawn (shrimp) paste	$^1/_2$ tsp, roasted and crumbled
Coriander seeds	$^1/_2$ tsp, crushed
Cooking oil	2 Tbsp
Cassava leaves	200 g, cleaned and blanched for 5 minutes and roughly chopped
Bamboo skewers	
Banana leaves	
String	

Method

- Season inside and outside of duck with salt and pepper.

- Combine all ingredients except cassava leaves, bamboo skewers and banana leaves and mix thoroughly. Set a quarter of this mixture aside.

- Combine remaining mixture with cassava leaves and stuff into cavity of duck. Secure opening with a bamboo skewer.

- Rub outside of duck with reserved mixture, then wrap duck in several layers of banana leaves. Fasten with string.

- Steam parcel for 50 minutes then transfer duck parcel to an oven and roast at 180°C for a further 30–40 minutes.

Soy Beans (Kedele)

Soy beans are one of the most versatile foods. They can be boiled, fried or steamed as they are, or processed to produce other edible products. Soy bean oil is widely used in cooking and food processing. Soy bean sprouts, known in Bali as *utik-utik*, is eaten as a vegetable just like mung bean sprouts (*kacang ijo*). When ground, the soy beans produce soy bean milk which is now commonly available in Bali, in a variety of flavours. Fermented soy beans also form the basis of one of the most important Asian condiments, known as soy sauce or *kecap* in Indonesia. This sauce is available in two varieties: sweetened with sugar (*kecap manis*) or salted (*kecap asin*).

Bean curd or tofu is another product of soy beans. This is a soft jelly-like cake made from curdled soy bean milk. Yet another product is *tempe*, a soy bean cake native to Indonesia. Cooked soy beans are fermented with the help of an edible fungus to form a firm white cake. *Tempe* is used in many dishes in Indonesia.

Eggs

Eggs form an important part of the Balinese diet because they are readily available, cheap, and, in the belief of many Balinese people, a good substitute for meat or fish. In Bali, one would not expect to find any meat or fish dish in an average home meal if there is an egg dish and vice versa.

As refrigeration is not widespread in Bali, the shelf life of eggs in this hot, humid climate tends to be limited. To prevent any wastage, surplus eggs are preserved in two ways: *mauyah* and *asin. Mauyah* refers to salting the eggs. Using this method, the eggs are washed then boiled for up to eight hours in a liquid by-product of *arak.* (This by-product can be obtained cheaply from the rice wine distilleries.) While the eggs are still warm, they are put into a strainer where a mash of cassava starch, salt and water is dripped onto the eggs to coat the shell and then left to dry. Eggs put through this treatment will keep for up to two weeks. The other method is more complex and eggs thus treated are known as *taluh asin* or *taluh bekasem.* The eggs are washed thoroughly then coated with a muddy mixture of kitchen ashes, salt, red cement, brick powder and vinegar. The coated eggs are put into a large open woven basket and left for about two weeks. It is believed that the longer the eggs remain coated, the better they will taste. However, they are also believed to become salty if left coated for too long. When cracked open, the eggs are black and they get darker the longer they are kept.

Fried Bean Curd in Turmeric Coconut Dressing
Tahu Kalas Serves 4

Ingredients

Bean curd	4 pieces, each 100 g, sliced
Rice flour	2 Tbsp
Cooking oil for deep-frying	
Spice paste for vegetables	60 g (see pg 30)
Salam leaf	1
Kaffir lime leaves	2
Lemon grass	1 stalk, bruised
Bird's eye chillies	1–3, bruised
Vegetables or chicken stock	375 ml (see pg 41)
Coconut cream	180 ml
Salt	to taste
White peppercorns	2–3, finely crushed
Lime juice	1 Tbsp

Method

- Dust sliced bean curd evenly with rice flour, then deep-fry in medium hot oil until crisp. Set aside.

- In a saucepan, heat 1 Tbsp oil. Add spice paste and sauté until fragrant. Add *salam* leaf, kaffir lime leaves, lemon grass and bird's eye chillies and continue to sauté for another 1 minute.

- Pour in stock and coconut cream. Bring to the boil and simmer until sauce is slightly thickened.

- Add fried bean curd slices, gently mix, and season to taste with salt, pepper and lime juice.

Fermented Soy Bean Cake in Sweet Soy Sauce
Sambal Goreng Tempe Serves 4

Ingredients

Coconut oil	2 Tbsp
Shallots	60 g, peeled and sliced
Garlic	40 g, peeled and sliced
Large red chillies	40 g, seeded and finely sliced
Galangal	30 g, peeled and sliced
Palm sugar	20 g, chopped
Sweet soy sauce	3 Tbsp
Vegetable or chicken stock	3 Tbsp (see pg 41)
Tomato	1, skinned, seeded and cut into strips
Fermented soy bean cake	200 g, cut in long narrow strips and crisp-fried
Salt	a pinch
Bird's eye chillies	4, chopped (optional)

Method

- Heat oil in frying pan (skillet), add shallots, garlic, chillies and galangal and sauté for 2–4 minutes.

- Add palm sugar and sweet soy sauce and continue to sauté until evenly glazed. Add stock and bring to the boil. Add tomato and continue to sauté for 1 more minute.

- Add fermented soy bean cake and stir frequently until the sauce has reduced and caramelised.

- Season to taste with salt and stir in bird's eye chillies just before serving if desired.

From top: Fried Bean Curd in Turmeric Coconut Dressing; Fermented Soy Bean Cake in Sweet Soy Sauce

Eggs in Coconut Garlic Dressing

Telor Sambal Kesuna Serves 4

Ingredients

Coconut oil	2 Tbsp
Hardboiled eggs	4, shelled
Garlic	40 g, peeled and sliced
Large red chillies	40 g, seeded and finely sliced
Spice paste for chicken	60 g (see pg 31)
Lemon grass	1 stalk, bruised
Salam leaves	2
Chicken stock	125 ml (see pg 41)
Coconut cream	250 ml
Salt	a pinch

Method

- Heat oil in a frying pan (skillet), add hardboiled eggs and fry for 5 minutes until golden. Drain eggs and keep warm.

- In the same pan, sauté garlic and chillies until lightly browned. Add spice paste and sauté until fragrant.

- Add lemon grass, *salam* leaves and stock and bring to the boil. Add coconut cream and eggs and return to the boil then simmer over very low heat until sauce is slightly thickened. Season to taste with salt.

Eggs in Spiced Tomato Sauce

Telor Base Lalah Serves 4

Ingredients

Garlic	20 g, peeled and sliced
Dried prawn (shrimp) paste	$1/2$ tsp, roasted and crumbled
Large red chillies	50 g, seeded and sliced
Bird's eye chillies	3–5, sliced
Tomatoes	100 g, seeded and sliced
Coconut oil	2 Tbsp
Salt	a pinch
Hardboiled eggs	4, shelled

Method

- Combine garlic, dried prawn paste, chillies and tomatoes in a food processor or stone mortar and grind into a very fine paste.

- Heat oil in frying pan (skillet), add ground paste and cook over medium heat for 5 minutes. Season to taste with salt.

- Slice the eggs in half and top with sauce.

From top: Eggs in Coconut Garlic Dressing; Eggs in Spiced Tomato Sauce

Rice

Rice is not just important in the food culture of Bali—it is central. Rice is not just an accompaniment to other foods—it is the main dish and other side dishes accompany it. In fact, most Balinese people use the words "rice" and "food" interchangeably. An invitation to eat is commonly "Let's go have rice". Rice is sometimes called "Dewa" or "I Dewa", "God". Rice is the *sekala* (tangible) form of Dewi Sri, the Goddess of rice, wife of Visnu, together with whom she represents beauty, fertility, maintenance of life, and all that is necessary and good in the Balinese cosmos. The double triangle-shaped chilli, Bali's most popular symbol, is a representation of Dewi Sri. She is the object of countless prayers and ceremonies.

Rice is so important in the lives of the Balinese that all civil servants are given part of their salaries in the form of rice. Each government employee receives an allowance of 10 kg of rice per month. If the employee is married, the allowance is increased to 20 kg. And each child, up to and including three, receives a 10 kg ration. The maximum is 50 kg per family per month, a subtle message to encourage family planning. While 10 kg of rice is not really enough for one person per month, it does help to elevate some of the financial burden on a family. Most Balinese eat about 1.5 kg of rice per day. The weight is measured in terms of *baas* (uncooked rice) not *nasi* (cooked rice).

Types of Rice

Baas Bali is an old style rice that is falling out of favour because of its low yield, long growing season and susceptibility to insects. Most Balinese, however, agree that it is the best tasting rice. *Baas* Bali is a graceful plant that grows as tall as a man, with mature heads that bend over at the top. The grains are short and fat, and they cost 50 per cent more than regular types of rice.

Most of the other types of rice planted in Bali are dwarf varieties, sometimes collectively referred to as "new" rice. These dwarf strains were developed to cultivate high yield, insect resistant rice with short growing seasons. Although these plants are not as graceful as the older varieties, the fact that Indonesia has turned from an importer of rice to become self-sufficient in the last couple of decades is testimony to the fact that dwarf rice stains have saved the day. These varieties of rice are known by such names as Sedani, C4, PB6 and IR36, the meanings of which are not known to most people.

Black and red rice are also grown in Bali. They are known as *padi injin* (black rice) and *padi barak* (red rice). Although only the outer surface of the grain is coloured, the entire grain takes on the colour when it is cooked.

The Balinese place special emphasis on colours and colour symbolism. Thus, it is significant to them that the three natural colours of rice correspond to the colours that symbolise three of the four cardinal directions and their respective Gods. Black is symbolic of Betara Wisnu in the north, white represents Betara Iswara in the east and red, Betara Brahma in the south. Only yellow, the colour of Betara Mahadewa in the west, is lacking. This is however compensated for by using turmeric, which the Balinese believe was given to them by the Gods so they would have all four colours. Rice of the four colours are often given as offerings. Such offerings have to be orientated with the colours in the proper directions. In the centre is placed a mixture of all four colours. Called *brunbun*, this represents the God, Betara Siwa.

Black and red rice are not used in the same way as regular rice because they are expensive and because they are glutinous (sticky) when cooked. (Another type of glutinous rice that is white in colour is called *ketan*.) When glutinous rice is boiled or steamed, the grains stick together. The Balinese insist upon having their rice for meals fluffy, with each grain separate, and so red, black or sticky rice would not meet their preference. Sticky rice is instead used for making cakes, puddings and *arak*.

Cooking Rice

Three basic pieces of equipment are required when making *nasi kuskus*, steamed rice. First, water is boiled in an hour glass shaped container called a *dangdang*. The *dangdang* is almost always made of sheet iron that has crimped and soldered joints. Some aluminium ones are available but are more expensive. The base of the common *dangdang* is about 30-cm in diameter. The side slopes inward to form a narrow neck of about 20-cm, then flares abruptly outward to open up at the top. This mouth of the *dangdang* is about the same size as the base. The *panguskusan*, the rice steamer, is shaped like a cone, and it nests in the mouth of the *dangdang*. It is made from bamboo strips woven in such a way that the part near the bottom of the cone has small gaps between the strips so steam can pass through. (I have seen many tourists wearing the *panguskusan* as a hat, much to the amusement of the Balinese!) The rice to be steamed is placed into the *panguskusan* and covered with a clay lid called the *kekeb*. The *kekeb* keeps the steam from escaping too rapidly.

Ketipat (Rice Cakes)

Rice is sometimes prepared in the form of *ketipat*, where it is placed into an *urung*, a small container woven from pale green coconut leaves and then boiled. There are many different varieties and shapes of *ketipat*, each with a different name and purpose. The more exotic and unusual shapes are used exclusively for religious ceremonies, while the most common type, known as *ketipat nasi, ketipat biasa* or *ketipat bekel*, is simply a flattened square pocket about 8-cm in size.

There are various reasons for making *ketipat*. For one, rice cooked in leaves is always a bit softer then ordinary steamed or boiled rice. Secondly, they are also easy to carry around. Farmers commonly bring *ketipat* out to the fields as meals and snacks, and street food sellers who do not wish to cook rice on the spot also commonly carry *ketipat* with them. Thirdly, *ketipat* can be somewhat overcooked so that it is soft and easy to digest by older people. This variation is known as *ketipat nyaling*, meaning "slippery". Ordinarily, when rice is overcooked, it becomes soft and mushy, like porridge. However, when it is cooked in an *urung*, the result is soft rice. It is not clear to anyone why this is so, but perhaps it has to do with the confined space in which the rice cooks when put into an *urung*. Fourthly, *ketipat* are pretty. The Balinese like to make and use them for aesthetic reasons.

To make *ketipat*, the rice is washed and filled into *urungs* until each one is half full. The parcels are then boiled for about an hour or until no water runs out of the parcels when you lift them up out of the boiling water. *Ketipat* are never steamed. As with ordinary rice, *ketipat* does not keep longer than about 12 hours before it starts to smell bad and taste sour.

Yellow Rice

Nasi Kuning Serves 4–5

To the Balinese, yellow is a festive colour, so yellow rice is an important part of every ceremonial feast.

Ingredients

Long grain rice	**250 g**

Dressing

Coconut oil	**1 Tbsp**
Shallots	**50 g, peeled and chopped**
Garlic	**25 g, peeled and chopped**
Chicken stock	**500 ml (see pg 41)**
Coconut cream	**250 ml**
Lemon grass	**1 stalk, bruised**
***Salam* leaves**	**2**
Screwpine (*pandan*) leaf	**1**
Turmeric water	**3 Tbsp (see pg 38)**
Salt	**a pinch**

Method

- Clean and rinse rice well under running water, then soak in fresh water for 25 minutes. Drain water and place rice into a conventional rice steamer to steam for 25 minutes.

- Meanwhile prepare dressing. Heat oil in a saucepan and sauté shallots and garlic for 1 minute. Add all other ingredients, bring to the boil, lower heat and simmer for 5 minutes.

- Pour steamed rice into a deep bowl and add boiling dressing over. Mix well and allow rice to absorb liquid. Return rice to steamer and steam for another 25 minutes or until rice is done.

Steamed Rice

Nasi Putih Serves 7–8

Ingredients

Long grain rice	**450 g**

Method

- Clean and rinse rice well under running water, then soak in fresh water for 25 minutes. Drain water and place rice into a conventional rice steamer to steam for 25 minutes.

- Remove rice from steamer, place into a deep bowl and fill with boiling water. Allow rice to absorb water for 5 minutes.

- Return rice to the steamer and steam again for about 25 minutes or until cooked. Lower heat and keep rice warm in the steamer before serving.

Note:
The conventional rice steamer can simply be a pot standing over boiling water in a larger, covered pot or steamer.

Fried Rice

Nasi Goreng Serves 4

Although it is not often prepared in private homes, nasi goreng *is a very popular restaurant treat for the Balinese. Each restaurant and cook would have a different way of preparing* nasi goreng, *but it is commonly cooked using only cold rice and very little oil. You can order it mixed up with almost any kind of meat or vegetables and you may also get a few pieces of fried chicken or some skewers of* sate *on the side. In Bali,* nasi goreng *is often served topped with a fried egg.*

Ingredients

Coconut oil	6 Tbsp
Shallots	6, peeled, halved and sliced
Garlic	6 cloves, peeled and sliced
Carrot	1, sliced into fine strips
Large red chillies	2, halved, seeded and finely sliced
Bird's eye chillies	2, sliced (optional)
White cabbage	100 g, sliced into fine strips
Spiced tomato sauce	1 Tbsp (see pg 32)
Chicken legs	200 g, diced
Light soy sauce	2 Tbsp
Eggs	2, beaten
Cooked rice	600 g, chilled
Celery	25 g, sliced
Leek	50 g, sliced
Spinach	50 g, cut into 2-cm lengths
Salt	a pinch
Fried shallots	2 Tbsp (see pg 37)

Method

- Heat oil in a wok or heavy frying pan (skillet). Add shallots, garlic, carrot and chillies and sauté for 1 minute until shallots and garlic are golden brown.

- Add cabbage, spiced tomato sauce and chicken and sauté for another 1 minute. Season with soy sauce and sauté until dry.

- Add eggs and scramble then add rice. Cook for another 3 minutes then add remaining ingredients except fried shallots. Mix well and season to taste with salt as necessary. Garnish with fried shallots.

Snacks

The Balinese are great snackers. Snacking makes up about a third of the daily food intake of the average Balinese. A casual trip trough any village reveals the truth of snacking. Wherever Balinese people gather to chat, test their fighting cocks, perform their obligatory group work functions, have *banjar* meetings, wash, pray or celebrate, there you will find many *warung* and their eager customers. A visit to almost any home compound, except during the hottest part of the day, will reveal children munching on a snack.

Snack sellers even penetrate the inner sanctums of offices, government or otherwise. Once, when I was at the governor's office, a snack vendor walked in and set his metal box down. All work came to a standstill for several minutes while the office personnel crowded around to choose and purchase their snacks.

Warung can also be found in every village neighbourhood, doubling up as fast food stores and social centres. People meet at *warungs* to swap stories or be updated with the local gossip. Families also make announcements of daughters that have reached marriageable age there. Besides the *warung* there are the pushcart vendors. If you wait long enough, one will surely come by your front door.

In Bali, snacks are known as *jaja*, and the word basically refers to any kind of food that is not eaten with rice or with the regular meal. Plain white bakery bread, chips, crackers and cookies are *jaja*.

Jaja may be prepared by any three cooking methods: frying, steaming or boiling, and it is typically made from three basic ingredients: coconut, palm sugar and rice. Coconut gives it flavour, palm sugar makes it sweet and rice holds it all together. There are two important varieties of rice that are used—ordinary and glutinous rice. Both varieties are available for sale in village markets either as whole grains or as flour. Most Balinese buy the whole grains and pound them into flour with a large rice pounder, like a giant mortar and pestle, made of wood, since it is cheaper than buying the ready ground flour.

Today, some *jaja* sellers work for a central supplier, instead of making the *jaja* themselves. These suppliers operate from large kitchens equipped with modern electric appliances, turning out large quantities of *jaja*, often packaged in plastic. This causes some of the authenticity of the process to be lost, but it is admittedly more sanitary.

In many village markets, the *jaja* sellers still make a few simple types of *jaja* at their stalls for sale. Most of these items sell out by early morning, so to experience the full range of items, you have to be there very early in the morning.

Fried Mashed Bananas
Jaja Pulung Biu Serves 4

This is a very delicious way to use up all your overripe bananas. For this reason, many warungs serve this snack together with a piping hot and very sweet coffee as an early morning bite.

Ingredients

Very ripe bananas	300 g, peeled
Plain (all-purpose) flour	100 g
Salt	1/4 tsp
Sugar	1 Tbsp
Cooking oil for deep-frying	

Method

- Mash bananas with a fork into a smooth paste. Add flour, salt and sugar and whisk into a soft elastic dough.

- Heat oil until very hot. Gently drop 1 heaped Tbsp of this dough into hot oil and deep-fry until crisp and golden. Continue until mixture is used up. Drain well.

Fried Bananas
Godoh Biu Serves 4

Fried bananas in batter are popular all over Asia. In Bali, they are generally called godoh biu. Biu dangsaba, *a variety of banana is preferred for this purpose. Pieces of the peeled bananas are dipped into a batter of rice flour and lime. The slices are then fried until golden brown in coconut oil. Besides banana, other ingredients used are sweet potatoes* (godoh kesela), *breadfruit* (godoh sukun) *or jackfruit* (godoh nangka). *They are delicious when freshly made and still warm, but as they keep relatively well, they are also often eaten as cold snacks.*

Ingredients

Rice flour	100 g
Plain (all-purpose) flour	50 g
Water	160 ml
Salt	a pinch
Finger bananas	8, peeled and sliced in half or 4 large bananas, peeled and sliced
Cooking oil for deep-frying	

Method

- Combine both types of flour, water and salt in a deep mixing bowl. Whisk until batter is smooth and slightly thick.

- Dip banana slices into batter and coat generously.

- Heat oil in a heavy saucepan. Place bananas into hot oil one at a time to prevent them from sticking together. Deep-fry bananas over low heat. Allow bananas to fry very slowly until golden brown and crisp.

- Drain well. Serve with palm sugar syrup (see pg 41) or coconut cream.

From top: Fried Mashed Bananas; Fried Bananas

Boiled Tubers

Umbi-umbian Serves 4

In Bali, when tubers are cooked for a main meal, some extra is prepared and left in the kitchen so family members can help themselves to it whenever they feel hungry.

Ingredients

Sweet potatoes, cassava or taro	**600 g, cleaned**
Grated coconut	**120 g**
Palm sugar syrup	**180 ml (see pg 41)**

Method

- Boil tubers in lightly salted water until tender. Drain water, peel and discard skin.

- Slice tubers evenly. (The tubers will break up into smaller pieces as you cut them.)

- Sprinkle with grated coconut and drizzle with palm sugar syrup before serving.

Sweet Corn and Coconut Snack

Urab Jagung Serves 4

This simple and very delicious snack is often eaten for breakfast together with a glass of piping hot Balinese coffee. Lentils, soy beans and various other beans are also prepared the same way.

Ingredients

Sweet corn kernels	**600 g, steamed**
Grated coconut	**120 g**
Sugar	**125 g**
Salt	**a pinch**
Coconut cream	**200 ml**

Method

- Combine sweet corn, coconut, sugar and salt and mix well. Serve drizzled with coconut cream.

From top: Boiled Tubers; Sweet Corn and Coconut Snack

Coconut Pancake

Dadar Serves 4

This pancake, with a sweet coconut filling known as unti, *is a popular snack food. It is sometimes eaten for breakfast.*

Ingredients

Rice flour	**100 g**
Sugar	**2 Tbsp**
Salt	**a pinch**
Eggs	**3**
Coconut cream	**250 ml**
Cooking oil	**2 Tbsp**

Coconut Filling

Palm sugar syrup	**125 ml (see pg 41)**
Grated coconut	**120 g**
Screwpine (**pandan**) **leaf**	**1**

Method

- Combine rice flour, sugar, salt, eggs, coconut cream and coconut oil in a deep mixing bowl. Stir well with a whisk until free of lumps. Pass through a strainer. Batter should be very liquid in consistency.

- Heat a non-stick pan over a low fire. Pour in 4 Tbsp mixture to form a very thin pancake. Continue until mixture is used up. Cool pancakes down to room temperature.

- Prepare the filling. Heat palm sugar syrup in a frying pan (skillet), add grated coconut and screwpine leaf and mix well over low heat for 2 minutes. Cool to room temperature.

- Place 1 Tbsp of coconut filling in the centre of a pancake. Using both hands, fold in 2 opposite edges of the pancake to enclose filling, then roll up, starting from the open edge closest to you. Continue to make more pancake rolls until ingredients are used up.

Glutinous Rice Cake
Wajik Serves 4

Ingredients

Glutinous white rice	375 g
Screwpine (*pandan*) **leaf**	1, knotted
Water	125 ml
Coconut cream	125 ml
Palm sugar	125 g
Salt	a pinch
Grated coconut	

Method

- Rinse rice under running water for 2 minutes, then soak for 4 hours. Rinse again until water runs clear. Place rice with screwpine leaf into a conventional steamer and steam for 30 minutes.

- Meanwhile, combine water, coconut cream and palm sugar and bring to the boil. Simmer for 2 minutes.

- Once rice is cooked, transfer to a deep bowl, add coconut cream mixture and salt and mix well until all liquid is absorbed. Spread rice evenly onto a baking tray, creating a 2.5-cm thick layer. Leave to cool to room temperature.

- Wet a sharp knife with warm water and cut rice into diamond shapes. To serve, sprinkle with grated coconut.

Note:
Instead of cooling and cutting the rice into cakes, you can also do it the traditional Balinese way. Take 1 heaped Tbsp of the mixture and shape into dumplings by hand.

Green Bean Pudding

Bubuh Kacang Ijo Serves 4

Bubuh *is a porridge made from rice flour or one of several pulses, such as mung beans. The rice flour or pulse is boiled in water until the desired consistency before various flavouring and colouring are added. The favourite additive used is derived from the leaves of a common plant called* kayu sughi. *The leaves are kneaded and squeezed in a little water and a pinch of lime is added to take away the green leafy taste that the Balinese call* engab. *The* kayu sughi *extract imparts a lovely green colour and flavour to* bubuh *and can also be used with other foods.*

Bubuh *is commonly made at home as a snack and it is also easily available from push cart vendors. These vendors announce their arrival by ringing bells or hitting something to make a loud noise. To purchase something from these vendors, people usually shout out to them from the house and the vendors would come into the compound of the house or park out front to dispense their snacks. You may bring your own dish for them to fill if you so wish. In many places, vendors arrive regularly every afternoon at 4 pm, and both young and old indulge for only a few rupiahs per serving.*

Ingredients

Mung beans	350 g
Water	1.5 litres
Ginger	50 g, peeled, sliced, and crushed
Coconut milk	500 ml
Sugar	125 g
Salt	a pinch

Method

- Remove husks from mung beans and pick out any broken beans and impurities. If preferred, heighten the flavour of the mung beans by heating them briefly in a stainless steel pan without oil. Be careful not to burn them.

- Wash beans thoroughly 2–3 times. Place in a pot and pour in water. Add ginger and bring to the boil. Simmer for about 30 minutes or until beans are tender then add coconut cream, sugar and salt and continue to simmer for another 10 minutes. Serve warm.

Dumplings in Palm Sugar Coconut Sauce

Jaja Batun Bedil Serves 4

Ingredients

Dumplings

Glutinous rice flour	150 g
Tapioca flour	60 g
Salt	a pinch
Water	180 ml

Sauce

Water	125 ml
Coconut cream	125 ml
Palm sugar	125 g, chopped
Screwpine (*pandan*) leaf	1, bruised
Salt	a pinch

Grated coconut
Coconut cream

Method

- For the dumplings, place rice flour, tapioca flour and salt into a deep mixing bowl. Gradually add water and mix well. Knead into a smooth dough. The dough should not be too dry but soft and elastic. Roll dough into small dumplings approximately 1-cm in diameter.

- In a saucepan, bring 4 litres of lightly salted water to the boil. Add dumplings and bring back to the boil then simmer for 5 minutes. Drain and cool dumplings in ice water.

- For the sauce, combine all ingredients and bring to the boil, stirring. Simmer for 5 minutes.

- Add dumplings to the sauce and simmer over very low heat for 20 minutes. Cool and serve at room temperature together with grated coconut and coconut cream.

Steamed Pumpkin Cake

Sumping Waluh Makes 20

Ingredients

Pumpkin	500 g, peeled and finely shredded
Grated coconut	250 g
Rice flour	150 g
Sugar	100 g
Salt	1 tsp
Banana leaves	20, each cut into 18 x 22-cm sheets

Method

- Combine pumpkin, grated coconut, rice flour, sugar and salt into a smooth dough.

- Break the fibres of the banana leaves to allow for easy folding. Do this by steaming the leaves for 10 seconds, placing them over an open gas flame for 5 seconds or cooking them in the microwave oven for 3 seconds on HIGH.

- Place 2 heaped Tbsp pumpkin filling in the centre of a banana leaf and fold long edges of banana leaf in towards each other. Bend open ends back and tuck under parcel. Continue until mixture is used up. Steam parcels for 25 minutes. Cool to room temperature before serving.

Black Rice Pudding
Bubuh Injin Serves 4

Ingredients

Black glutinous rice	**250 g**
White glutinous rice	**75 g**
Screwpine (*pandan*) leaf	**1**
Water	**1.25 litres**
Palm sugar syrup	**175 ml (see pg 41)**
Salt	**a pinch**
Coconut cream	**375 ml**

Method

- Rinse black and white glutinous rice well under running water. Soak overnight. Drain before using.

- Place 750 ml of water, black and white glutinous rice and screwpine leaf into a heavy pan and simmer over medium heat for approximately 45 minutes. Add more water as necessary.

- Add palm sugar syrup and continue to cook until almost all liquid has evaporated. Season with a pinch of salt then remove from heat and leave to cool. Serve at room temperature, topped with coconut cream.

> **Tip:** Follow this same recipe to make steamed sticky rice cake (*jaja kuskus*), but double the amount of glutinous white rice used and omit the black glutinous rice.

Steamed Black Rice with Coconut
Jaja Injin Serves 4

This delicious but simple snack is often served for breakfast together with a glass of thick, black and very sweet coffee.

Ingredients

Black glutinous rice	**175 g**
White glutinous rice	**175 g**
Screwpine (*pandan*) leaves	**3**
Grated coconut	**120 g**
Palm sugar syrup	**125 ml (see pg 41)**
Coconut cream	**250 ml**

Method

- Rinse black and white glutinous rice well under running water. Soak overnight. Drain before using.

- Place black and white glutinous rice together with screwpine leaves into a conventional steamer and steam for approximately 45 minutes or until rice is soft.

- Spoon rice onto a flat tray and season with a pinch of salt. Leave to cool.

- Just before serving, stir grated coconut and palm sugar syrup into rice. Serve at room temperature with coconut cream on the side.

From top: Black Rice Pudding; Steamed Black Rice with Coconut

Fried Yam Doughnuts with Palm Sugar

Onde Onde Makes 10

Ingredients

Yam	500 g, peeled and finely shredded
Salt	1 tsp
Palm sugar	100 g
White sesame seeds	50 g
Cooking oil for deep-frying	

Method

- Combine yam and salt and knead into a smooth dough.

- Form dough into small balls about 3-cm in diameter. With your finger, make a deep cavity in each ball and insert 10 g of palm sugar. Enclose palm sugar by folding dough over opening. Roll again with your hands into balls then coat evenly with sesame seeds.

- Deep-fry in medium hot oil until lightly browned. Drain and cool to room temperature before serving.

Note:

If the yam dough is too soft or watery, gradually knead in some rice flour before proceeding.

Finger Bananas in Coconut Cream

Kolek Pisang Serves 4–6

Ingredients

Palm sugar syrup	500 ml (see pg 41)
Screwpine (*pandan*) leaf	1, knotted
Salt	a pinch
Finger bananas	16, peeled and each cut into half lengthwise
Corn flour (cornstarch) (optional)	1 Tbsp, mixed with 1 Tbsp water
Lime juice	2 Tbsp
Coconut cream	125 ml

Method

- Place palm sugar syrup, screwpine leaf and salt in a saucepan. Bring to the boil over medium heat and simmer for 5 minutes.

- Add finger bananas, reduce heat to low and continue to simmer for another 5 minutes.

- Should syrup be too thin for your preference, stir corn flour paste into syrup. Simmer for a few more minutes then remove from heat.

- Discard screwpine leaf, add lime juice and leave to cool. Serve warm or at room temperature with coconut cream on the side.

This page:

Lemon grass *(Sere)*

Facing page, from top left to right:

Kaffir lime leaves *(Don juuk purut)*

Limes *(Limau)*

Bilimbi *(Belimbing buluh)*

Screwpine (*pandan***) leaves** *(Don pandan harum)*

Lemon basil *(Don kemangi)*

Large red chillies *(Tabia Lombok)*

Red chillies *(Tabia merah)*

Small chillies *(Tabia Bali)*

Shallots *(Bawang merah/Allium bawang)*

Salam leaves *(Don salam)*

Turmeric *(Kunyit)*

Ginger *(Jahe)*

Galangal *(Isen)*

Lesser galangal *(Cekuh)*

Nutmeg *(Jebug garum)*

Candlenuts *(Tingkih)*

Peanuts (Groundnuts) *(Kacang tanah)*

Tamarind *(Celagi/Lunak)*

Prawn (shrimp) paste *(Terasi)*

Palm sugar *(Gula barak/Gula Bali)*

Cloves *(Cengkeh)*

Black rice *(Injin)*

Red rice *(Baas merah)*

Black peppercorns *(Mica selem)*

Coriander seeds *(Ketumbah)*

Common Ingredients

Bilimbi (*Belimbing buluh*)
This small green fruit is extremely sour and is used almost entirely as a flavouring in Bali. It is also known as sour finger carambola or small sour starfruit. If not available, replace with segments of lime.

Black rice (*Injin*)
Black glutinous rice is commonly used for making cakes and puddings served with palm sugar and coconut cream. The short, round grains are black on the outside but white in the centre. They are considerably more expensive than ordinary white rice. In the fields, black rice looks similar to white rice.

Candlenut (*Tingkih*)
Known as *kemiri* in Indonesia, this is a brittle, waxy yellowish nut that is similar in appearance to the macadamia nut. It is used as a binding agent and adds a faint flavour to dishes. If not available, use shelled and skinned raw peanuts.

Chillies
The Balinese love using chilli in their food and often use an excessive amount. Three types of chillies are used and the level of heat increases as the size decreases. Always wear gloves when handling chillies and wash hands and all surfaces in contact with the chillies thoroughly thereafter.

Large red chillies (*Tabia lombok*)
These finger-sized chillies are by far the mildest chillies found in Bali. They are mainly used for flavouring and are always seeded before use. Most recipes in this book make use of these chillies. If the chillies you use are hot, reduce the quantity by one-third.

Small chillies (*Tabia Bali*)
This short, fat chilli is only about 2.5 cm long and it is the most favoured and commonly used chilli. They are normally chopped or bruised before use, adding a good spicy kick to the dishes prepared.

Bird's eye chillies (*Tabia kerinyi*)
These tiny green chillies are the spiciest ones. They are mostly used raw to spice up condiments.

Cardamom (*Kapulaga*)
The strong, eucalyptus-like flavour of cardamom is not widely used in Balinese cooking except in some chicken and lamb dishes. The whitish coloured, fibrous pod encloses pungent black seeds, which release a very strong perfumed aroma when finely crushed in a stone mortar.

Cinnamon (*Mesui*)
This delicately fragrant, slightly sweet spice is native to Sri Lanka though it is now grown in most hot, wet, tropical regions. Most of the cinnamon sold in Bali is from the bark of the species Brummani which is grown in Sumatra. Try not to use ground cinnamon but rather the bark, which adds a much softer flavour to dishes.

Coconut (*Nyuh*)
Freshly grated coconut is perhaps the most used ingredient in Balinese cooking, from vegetable and meat dishes to cakes. Freshly grated coconut is now available vacuum-packed in supermarkets. Desiccated coconut moistened with coconut milk can be used as a substitute if freshly grated coconut is not available.

Coconut oil (*Lengis*)
This is the preferred oil in Balinese cooking. Most of the recipes in this book ask for it. Coconut oil is now commercially produced. It is cholesterol-free and very light, but might not be available outside Asia. Substitute with a light vegetable, peanut, sunflower or soy bean oil. Sesame and olive oil are not good substitutes as they are too strong and overpowering.

Coconut milk or cream (*Santan*)
Do not confuse this with coconut water, which is the clear liquid, inside the hollow of the coconut. *Santan* is a white milky liquid obtained by combining 240 g of freshly grated coconut with 500 ml of warm water. Stir the mixture thoroughly and leave to cool. Pour the liquid through two layers of muslin cloth or a potato shredder and squeeze to extract as much liquid as possible. Refrigerate the liquid for 30 minutes—the milk will separate from the cream. The cream can then be easily skimmed off. In Bali, the light cream is served with cakes and porridge and the milk is used to cook stews. Today, coconut milk and cream is available pre-packed in most Asian stores.

Clove (*Cengkeh*)
The clove tree is a member of the myrtle family and is native to Southeast Asia. It grows to 9 m in height and flourishes near the sea. The central mountain ranges of Bali are full of this very pretty reddish-coloured tree. The spice is the unopened flower bud. When dried, it turns a reddish-brown colour and becomes one of the strongest smelling spices. Indonesia is the largest producer and consumer of cloves but the spice is seldom used in Balinese cooking.

Coriander seeds (*Ketumbah*)
This dried spice is commonly used in Balinese cooking. They are crushed before use which imparts a much stronger flavour.

Galangal (*Isen*)
This large rhizome is a standard ingredient in Balinese cooking. It is known as *laos* in Indonesia and greater galangal in English. It is available fresh or in powder form in many Asian shops and supermarkets.

Lesser galangal (*Cekuh*)
A small rhizome that is a standard ingredient in Balinese cooking. It is called *kencur* in Indonesia and is available ground, in powder form. If unavailable, replace the amount required in a recipe with an equal amount of ginger and galangal.

Garlic (*Kesuna*)
The garlic used in Bali is similar to the common garlic but its cloves are usually smaller with a slightly less pungent flavour.

Ginger (*Jahe*)
The rhizome of an attractive flowering plant, ginger is widely used in Balinese cooking. Ginger should be plump and firm. Peel then either slice or pound before using. It is easily available in Asian stores and should never be substituted with ground ginger.

Lemon basil (*Don kemangi*)
This delicate herb has a very pleasant citrus flavour and is mostly used with fish dishes cooked in banana leaves. Regular basil can be used as a substitute.

Lemon grass (*Sere*)
A common ingredient in Balinese cooking, lemon grass must be peeled and lightly bruised before use, or bruised and very finely sliced. When used to flavour spice paste or sauce, bruise it along the whole length and tie into a knot. This will prevent the lemon grass fibres from falling apart. If lemon grass is unavailable, use lemon or lime zests.

Kaffir lime (*Juuk purut*)
This small green citrus fruit is often used in small quantities in Balinese cooking and also in traditional medicine. The fruit has a marked protrusion on one end and its skin is knobbly and wrinkled. Its taste ranges from sour to bitter and the Balinese prefer it to any other type of lime. The common lime found in most Asian shops makes an acceptable substitute.

Kaffir lime leaf (*Don juuk purut*)
The kaffir lime leaf looks like two leaves joined end to end and it is used whole in soups and sauces or finely chopped for fish, duck and chicken dishes.

Nutmeg (*Jebug garum*)
This aromatic sweet spice is mostly used with strong flavoured meats such as duck and lamb. Avoid using ready-ground nutmeg as it loses its flavour readily. Instead, grate whole nutmeg just before it is needed.

Palm sugar (*Gula barak* or *Gula Bali*)
Sold in cylindrical or round cakes, palm sugar is obtained by boiling the liquid extracted from the unopened flower bud of some palm trees, such as the sugar palm in Bali or the coconut tree in Java. In the northeastern part of Bali, palm sugar is made from the Lontar Palm. (This same liquid is also used to produce palm wine, if allowed to ferment.)

Peanuts (Groundnuts)
(*Kacang tanah*)
When choosing raw peanuts, look for those with the skin still on. Peanuts are tastier and more flavoursome when they are deep-fried or roasted in their skins. The second best thing is peanuts which are roasted in the shell. These are available in most supermarkets.

Pepper (*Mica puthi* or *mica selem*)
In Balinese cooking, black pepper is more popularly used than white pepper. Grind or crush fresh peppercorns, as ground pepper looses its aroma quickly.

Salam leaf (*Don salam*)
The *salam* leaf is used to flavour soups, stews, vegetable and meat dishes. Although similar to the bay leaf in use and appearance, they are completely different and should not be used as substitutes for each other.

Screwpine (*pandan*) **leaf**
(*Don pandan harum*)
The aromatic leaf of a type of almost thornless *pandanus*, the screwpine leaf is used for flavouring cakes and snacks. The shredded leaf is also a common topping on offering baskets in Bali.

Shallots
(*Bawang merah, Allium bawang*)
The common onion available in Bali is small and red, and just slightly different from shallots sold in other parts of the world. If this type of shallot is not available, replace with red Spanish onions.

Prawn (shrimp) paste (*Terasi*)
Made by drying prawns under the sun and then pounding them into a pulp, this pungent paste is available in small packages from the market. Grill or roast without oil before using. Roasted prawn paste can be stored for several months in an airtight container. Although pungent, prawn paste adds a pleasant flavour when used in dishes.

Soy Sauce
(*Kecap Asin* and *Kecap Manis*)
Soy sauce may be salty (*asin*) or sweet (*manis*). Both varieties are served at the Balinese table. Salty soy sauce is commonly known outside Bali as light soy sauce.

Tamarind (*Celagi/Lunak*)
The tamarind seed pod ripens on the tree. It contains a fleshy pulp, which has a very sour taste. The pulp needs to be soaked in warm water for 15 minutes then strained through a fine sieve. The seed and fibres are then discarded. Only the juice is used. Tamarind is widely available in their pods or compressed, minus pods and seeds.

Turmeric (*Kunyit*)
An attractive perennial with large lily-like leaves and yellow flowers, turmeric is a member of the ginger family and, like ginger, it is an underground rhizome of the plant. The brownish skin must be scraped or peeled to expose the bright yellow flesh. If fresh turmeric is not available, substitute 1 Tbsp ground turmeric for 100 g fresh roots.

Weights & Measures

Quantities for this book are given in Metric and American (spoon) measures. Standard spoon measurements used are: 1 tsp = 5 ml and 1 Tbsp = 15 ml. All measures are level unless otherwise stated.

LIQUID AND VOLUME MEASURES

Metric	Imperial	American
5 ml	$^1/_6$ fl oz	1 teaspoon
10 ml	$^1/_3$ fl oz	1 dessertspoon
15 ml	$^1/_2$ fl oz	1 tablespoon
60 ml	2 fl oz	$^1/_4$ cup (4 tablespoons)
85 ml	$2^1/_2$ fl oz	$^1/_3$ cup
90 ml	3 fl oz	$^3/_8$ cup (6 tablespoons)
125 ml	4 fl oz	$^1/_2$ cup
180 ml	6 fl oz	$^3/_4$ cup
250 ml	8 fl oz	1 cup
300 ml	10 fl oz ($^1/_2$ pint)	$1^1/_4$ cups
375 ml	12 fl oz	$1^1/_2$ cups
435 ml	14 fl oz	$1^3/_4$ cups
500 ml	16 fl oz	2 cups
625 ml	20 fl oz (1 pint)	$2^1/_2$ cups
750 ml	24 fl oz ($1^1/_5$ pints)	3 cups
1 litre	32 fl oz ($1^3/_5$ pints)	4 cups
1.25 litres	40 fl oz (2 pints)	5 cups
1.5 litres	48 fl oz ($2^2/_5$ pints)	6 cups
2.5 litres	80 fl oz (4 pints)	10 cups

OVEN TEMPERATURE

	°C	°F	Gas Regulo
Very slow	120	250	1
Slow	150	300	2
Moderately slow	160	325	3
Moderate	180	350	4
Moderately hot	190/200	370/400	5/6
Hot	210/220	410/440	6/7
Very hot	230	450	8
Super hot	250/290	475/550	9/10

LENGTH

Metric	Imperial
0.5 cm	$^1/_4$ inch
1 cm	$^1/_2$ inch
1.5 cm	$^3/_4$ inch
2.5 cm	1 inch

DRY MEASURES

Metric	Imperial
30 grams	1 ounce
45 grams	$1^1/_2$ ounces
55 grams	2 ounces
70 grams	$2^1/_2$ ounces
85 grams	3 ounces
100 grams	$3^1/_2$ ounces
110 grams	4 ounces
125 grams	$4^1/_2$ ounces
140 grams	5 ounces
280 grams	10 ounces
450 grams	16 ounces (1 pound)
500 grams	1 pound, $1^1/_2$ ounces
700 grams	$1^1/_2$ pounds
800 grams	$1^3/_4$ pounds
1 kilogram	2 pounds, 3 ounces
1.5 kilograms	3 pounds, $4^1/_2$ ounces
2 kilograms	4 pounds, 6 ounces

ABBREVIATION

tsp	teaspoon
Tbsp	tablespoon
g	gram
kg	kilogram
ml	millilitre